THE LOVE CALL OF
HAROLD J. LIEBERMAN

Toby Elle

This book is dedicated to our grandchildren

Milo and Delilah

two good writers

Table of Contents

Preface

My husband, Harold J. Lieberman, through hard work, determination and help from mentors and therapists to overcome childhood traumas, was able to have a very interesting life and a wonderful career as a trumpet player in New York City (playing in both classical and jazz idioms). He was respected in the 1960's as one of most successful musicians in New York City, where he met many well known musicians and developed a collection of stories about his experiences.

While a member of the Arthur Godfrey radio show, Harold generated fan mail when he was featured playing a catchy tune written by the contractor, Gerry Alters, called, "The Love Call of Harold J. Lieberman." The song added variety to the usual Dixieland repertoire and spurred good natured banter amongst Arthur and the members of the band. It served a purpose then, and I decided to use it as the title of this book (just for fun) and to underscore Harold's general sense of humor that is part of his persona.

In his retirement Harold began lecturing to Life Long Learning groups of older adults in upstate New York, where his presentations were well crafted and full of personal and amusingly delivered anecdotes.

Harold thrived on the satisfaction that a variety of musical activities brought him, and you will see that he enjoyed the process of each step that led him to his goals. I guess you could call him an Everyman, but not just an average Joe, but an Everyman who persevered with single-mindedness and took each new path that presented itself.

Through the years family and friends urged Harold to write a book, but he never made it a priority. People have been very enthused about his lectures and some expressed their interest in his life, adding a new impetus to write about it. Now in his eighties and still having no motivation to do so, I have decided that I am the only logical person to tell his story, so let me begin.

Influence of a Dysfunctional Family

Harold was the fourth son born to Jennie and Jechiel Lieberman, Orthodox Jews who had come to America by way of Ellis Island in the 1920's, with their three-year-old son, Milton.

As a child, Jechiel had witnessed his father hanged on the porch by Russian Bolsheviks. As he heard his father yelling to him to get away, he ran into the woods where a bullet grazed his head. When he fell down he pretended to be dead and when the assassins left he ran back home. He never forgot this traumatic experience and longed to somehow live in a safer place, such as America.

As a young man Jechiel became very religious and studied the Torah diligently, establishing a reputation as a resource in matters of the Torah in his community. He decided it was time to move from his mother's home, but who would cook for him? In the kosher Orthodox home he would need a wife, and in his mind the best way to assure that he could count on the certainty of following the very specific Jewish law governing this matter, was to get an arranged marriage. The means to this goal was simply to consult with a matchmaker who had names of eligible young people desiring to marry, in order to carry on the laws of the Orthodox Jewish religion. The matchmaker Jechiel chose thought it suitable to pair the man who was considered the most learned in their town with the woman who would not only fulfill the requirements expected of an Orthodox Jewish wife, but was the most beautiful. The family of Jennie Steingart and Jennie herself approved of this match and the marriage took place.

Soon afterwards a son, Milton, was born. Three years later after careful planning and the knowledge that with the help of Polish Jewish friends he would be able to establish a life in Hartford, Connecticut, as a learned Jewish scholar and Hebrew teacher aligned with an Orthodox Synagogue, Jennie, Jechiel and Milton sailed to Ellis Island. Once in Hartford Jechiel was able to borrow money from a Jewish lending organization, which enabled him to purchase a house in the north section of Hartford where there were other Orthodox families. It didn't take long for Jechiel to locate used public school desks which he lined up in the living room, in order to teach the Torah to boys preparing for their Bar Mitzvahs.

Jennie fulfilled her role of keeping a kosher home and bore their second son, Benjamin in 1925, Louis, who died at an early age after falling out of his high chair and Harold, born in 1931.

The marriage was not a happy one. Besides teaching in the living room and sometimes counseling adults on religious or personal matters, Jechiel spent hours reading the Torah. Jennie had no real interest in his work. She often berated Jechiel in front of the children, saying in an angry voice, "You don't make enough money. Mr. Lipsy owns a gas station and he can afford to buy Mrs. Lipsy a fur coat!" When Jechiel became frustrated with her persistent nagging, his way of communicating was to smash a dish on the floor. There was constant tension in the home.

At dinner exemplary kosher meals were served, but when Jennie sucked the marrow out of a bone Benjamin sneered at her with disdain, loudly imitating the sound she was making. Milton might laugh, but Harold took second portions and focused on eating, which over time caused him to be overweight. He suppressed any feeling while looking down at his plate and noticing that his hands were sweating profusely. In fact, he noticed that his sweaty hands often sweated in school as well, causing the ink on his written work to smear. As a result, when his teachers couldn't read what he had written, they assumed he didn't know the answers. His grades reflected their opinions of him, and Harold began to feel that he was stupid. In an attempt to get to the bottom of the sweaty hands, Jennie routinely took him to a doctor who would give him a shot in his buttocks, which didn't help and only increased his humiliation and reinforced his low self-esteem. It was also during this difficult time that Harold began to stutter, an affliction that continued until many years later when he went to a therapist.

Because Harold's brother, Milton, was twelve years older than Harold, there was not much interaction between them. However, when Harold was twelve years old he told Milton, who played the double bass and was home on a break from the Eastman School of Music, that he wanted to play the drums. Milton offered to take Harold to the local music store where he hoped he might be inspired to consider other instruments as well. While there, the owner of the store, Mr. Perlmutter, was glad to see Milton and showed sincere interest in Harold's desire to play an instrument. Since he was a trumpet player, he took time to play the "William Tell Overture" (a familiar tune to many because of its use on *The Lone Ranger* radio show). Harold was spellbound and shortly after he began lessons with Mr. Perlmutter. Although his hands sweated, it was no hindrance to playing the instrument. In fact, this gave him confidence. Practicing became a refuge and he looked forward to practicing as often as possible. As he developed his skills, Mr. Perlmutter suggested that he play with the Hartt School of Music Youth Orchestra and begin studying with Gil Johnson, a gifted trumpet player and teacher at the school. This association was not only inspiring, but with Gil's guidance Harold became an outstanding player. The next step for him was to enroll in the Hartt School, which he did. When he was seventeen he auditioned and was hired as the principal trumpet player in the Hartford Symphony, playing the "Trumpeter's Lullaby" under guest conductor, Arthur Fiedler.

When Harold showed his parents a prominent article in the *Hartford Courant* newspaper mentioning his debut as a teenager with the Hartford Symphony, they were impressed, and Harold assumed they would go to the performance. His father was there, but Harold did not see his mother. When he got home, relishing his success, his mother was in the kitchen. He said, "Ma, why weren't you there?"

Jennie looked at Harold and said, "I couldn't go! You didn't give me a corsage!"

"Ma," Harold said dejectedly. "I'm sorry. I didn't know I should have given you a corsage."

"You couldn't even give me a corsage!" Jennie said with disgust.

After that exchange it was hard for Harold to hold on to the euphoria he experienced playing with the symphony. He went to his room and tried to go to sleep, listening to music on his crystal radio set.

Harold shared a room with Benny who was six years older, was valedictorian of his class and an accomplished clarinetist who could play like Benny Goodman. Occasionally he and Harold sat at the piano and Benny shared his knowledge of jazz with Harold. They listened to Benny's records of big bands and Benny took Harold to the State Theatre to hear bands that appeared there.

Harold began going to jam sessions where

other young musicians were trying to improve their improvisation skills, and he became very inspired and excited to excel.

By the time he was twenty-one years old, with Milton and Benny in the Army and one more year of the Hartt School to go before graduating, Harold found life at home so intolerable that he could no longer live there. He impulsively made a decision to join the Air Force.

Moving On

When Harold went down to the Hartford Air Force recruiting office, he went to the registration desk and said, "I want to enlist."

"O.K." said the clerk, "come back next week."

"No," Harold said emphatically. "I want to join now."

"Not many guys are that eager to join up," the clerk said, "but if that's what you wanna do, fill out these papers, pack a bag and come back tomorrow morning at 9:00 a.m. You can get on the bus that leaves from here going to Sampson Air Force Base where you'll do your basic training."

"Thanks," Harold said. "I'll be here!"

Harold was thrilled to be in the Air Force, especially during basic training when he exercised daily, lost weight and felt great. He wasn't happy when he was told that he was required to write a letter home, but he did the best he could.

Unfortunately, his problem with stuttering became worse and affected his trumpet playing. Similar to a stutterer trying to start a word, he had great difficulty in starting a note, unless someone gave him a visual cue. His tongue would freeze, blocking air into the mouthpiece.

After basic training, he was transferred to Westover Air Force Base in Massachusetts and assigned to the 730th AF Band. First Sgt. Lou (Goldie) Goldman (who had coincidently been Bar Mitzvahd by Harold's father) noticed his struggle, and when Harold told him that he wanted to see the principal trumpet player of the Boston Symphony for help Goldie was very sympathetic, issuing the necessary pass.

At the first meeting with Armando Ghitalla, who became Harold's third trumpet teacher, Ghitalla asked, "So what is it that you would like me to help you with?"

As Harold began his reply, nervously stuttering throughout, he said, "As you can obviously hear, I am a stutterer, but now I think it may be affecting my trumpet playing. I have trouble starting a note."

"Harold," Ghitalla, said, tears in his eyes, "I will be glad to give you trumpet lessons, but your problem is psychological and you need to see a psychologist. I had a similar problem when I was going to Juilliard, and Dr. Ruth Berenda, a lay analyst, greatly helped me. I can give you her phone number. I highly recommend her, and I think she can help you."

"I don't know what to think," Harold said. "I thought you might change my mouthpiece or embouchure. I have to say I'm really disappointed. I have to be able to play. I'll take her number, but I don't think I could see her in any event, since I'll be living on an air force base for the next four years."

"I wish I could help you, Harold,"

Ghitalla said. "I know what you're going through."

"Maybe my First Sgt. can work something out," Harold said dejectedly, shaking Ghitalla's hand. "I want to see you again," he said, hopefully.

"Call me any time," Ghitalla said.

When Harold got back to the base and had a chance to describe his encounter to Goldie, he couldn't believe his good fortune when Goldie was able to have him transferred to the band at McGuire Air Force Base in New Jersey, just one hour away from New York City. Even more amazing, Goldie secured permission for Harold to see Dr. Berenda on Tuesdays and Thursdays. This miraculous arrangement lasted until Harold's discharge in 1956.

With the wisdom and guidance of Dr. Berenda, Harold settled in New York City, and followed her advice to work on his image, mature and grow into a self-sufficient adult. He had been able to routinely study with Armando Ghitalla while still in New Jersey, and now in New York, and his difficulty with starting a note had slowly worked itself out. After taking certain psychological tests, Dr. Berenda was able to convince Harold that he wasn't stupid. With her encouragement, Harold auditioned and was accepted to Juilliard, from which he graduated.

As his therapy progressed, his self-esteem flourished and after a particularly dramatic session with Dr. Berenda and Harold's mother, his stuttering actually disappeared. In front of his therapist Harold felt free to confront his mother about her lack of regard for his feelings or pursuits, as well as her neglect of Eddie who died after falling out of a high chair. Hearing these raw accusations, Harold's mother stood up, clutching her purse and glaring at Harold with contempt. Her face reddened and was distorted in an ugly grimace, as she shouted,

"This is what you think? You're not getting a penny from me!" Harold rose to meet her gaze and said slowly and clearly without a stutter

"O.K., Ma!"

The session was over and an important milestone had been reached.

Becoming a Musician in New York City

In 1957, Harold became a member of the American Federation of Musicians, Local 802. To work as a musician in New York City he also had to have a mandatory New York City cabaret card, which could only be applied for at a Manhattan Police Station in lower Manhattan.[1]

At the police station, after Harold's records were checked, he was fingerprinted and told that the card would arrive in about six months. After completion of the humiliating fingerprinting process, the officer advised him to wash his blackened fingers in the men's room. Harold desperately needed the card to make some money as a trumpet player in New York City, and he had heard from other musicians that the

---

[1] This permit, which started during prohibition, was deactivated in 1967, when Frank Sinatra refused to apply for a cabaret card, saying that the application and investigation process was demeaning. As a result, the New York City Council voted 35-1 to eliminate the required cards. Unfortunately, prior to 1967, many great musicians and entertainers, such as Charlie Parker, Billie Holliday, Thelonius Monk and even Lenny Bruce were denied the card, resulting in the loss of their livelihood.

way to quickly get the card was to offer $25.00 cash to the officer in the men's room (also washing his fingers) with the hope that the issuance could be speeded up. It worked, and in three weeks Harold received his card.

As Harold had explained to me, on Mondays, Wednesdays and Fridays from 1:00-3:00, he would visit the "floor" (Roseland Ballroom on W. 52nd Street) where musicians, contractors and leaders would congregate to look for gigs and players for club dates (weddings, bar mitzvahs, parties, etc.). Resembling the New York Stock Exchange, musicians would enter the arena where an announcer with microphone sat at the front of the stage and might say, "Wanted, trumpet player (or other instrument) needed for Saturday night. Come to the front of the stage." Hearing this announcement, the player could approach the stage and signal to the announcer that he was interested. The announcer would point out the employer and the musician and employer would begin the bargaining process.

The "floor" was divided loosely into three areas. On the left (facing the stage) were jazz musicians who were looking for gigs that would allow them to play only jazz. These players knew the standard jazz tunes, but had little or no interest in learning and memorizing the more commercial club date repertoire (show tunes and ethnic dances). In the middle of the "floor" stood club date players looking for work in various catering halls and hotels in Manhattan, Brooklyn, the Bronx and Long Island. Since Saturday night was a premium night (busiest night for musicians to be employed) the free-lance club date musician, in an effort to obtain the most money, would barter his Saturday night to also include a weekday gig. The usual procedure began with the contractor saying, "I need a trumpet player for this Saturday. Are you open?" In order to get the best deal, the player would take out his or her date book and say, "Oh, I'm already booked, but

I might be able to get off. How much does it pay? (overtime, mileage, etc.) Do you have any other dates with it?"

The contractor would examine his large date book and say, "O.K., I'll throw in Tuesday at the Plaza Hotel with a possible overtime." The player might respond by saying, "O.K., I'll take it."

On the floor's right side were players who worked for the more sophisticated club date offices, i.e., Meyer Davis, Lester Lanin, Peter Duchin, etc. (At his peak Harold worked for those offices. His most memorable gig in that category was playing in Washington, D.C., at the Kennedy inauguration.) The repertoire for those bands was much more extensive and presented a big challenge for the players who kept abreast of the ever-changing Broadway Shows. The club date bands were either small combos or larger "big" bands consisting of three or four trumpets, three trombones and five saxes with piano, bass, drums and guitar and vocalists. Sheet music was never used and the players had to play "by ear." Those who were doublers (flugelhorn, flute, clarinet) were compensated. It was especially challenging for the non-solo players (second, third, fourth trumpet, trombone, second tenor sax, etc.) to make up the correct inner voice harmonies.

These highly skilled musicians made more money, as they received union wages plus mileage compensation to drive or fly to out of town affluent affairs.

The "floor" was not for the meek. At first being fearfully withdrawn, somewhat shy and reticent, it wasn't easy for Harold to adjust to the "New York" way of aggressiveness and bravado that he encountered. As he became more accustomed to the routine, he took risks and approached the stage a few times, being forced to learn to be more assertive.

During his weekly journey to the "floor"

Harold heard that someone was looking for a trumpet player to play in a Latin band. He met the band leader, Joe Quijano, who told him to come to a rehearsal somewhere in the Bronx. It turned out to be one of the most exciting and rewarding experiences (musically and socially) that he ever had. He was elated to know that all of the guys liked his playing and for the first time he felt wanted and accepted. The band had a steady Saturday night gig at the Taft Hotel on Broadway. If Joe called and Harold was available, he eagerly booked the date.

The sight of male Latin dancers dressed in bright colored shirts and women in colorful low cut dresses that showed off every curve and cleavage spontaneously doing the various steps of the Rhumba, Meringue, Mambo and Cha Cha Cha to the blaring sounds of the lively, frantic rhythms of Latin music was exhilarating for Harold and overwhelming to his senses. He felt as if he were riding on a roller coaster that would never come down to earth - round and round and round and round and round and he was being paid to do it - a lucky guy in New York City!

An important connection occurred when he heard the announcer on the "floor" blurt out,

"Wanted! Trumpet player for Kutcher's in the Catskills."

Harold approached the stage and the announcer pointed out the leader/ contractor, Danny Leroy (real name, Danny Lapedus). Harold went over to him and stated that he was interested in the job, as Danny suspiciously looked him over and asked him if he knew the tunes and could read a show.

Harold said that he had recently been honorably discharged from the U.S. Air Force Band and had a lot of experience playing shows and knew the "tunes." Danny said, "O.K., what key is 'I Could Have Danced All Night' in?" Harold wasn't sure and he said, "E flat." Danny replied, "Wrong! It's in the key of C." As he proceeded to walk away, Harold felt rather stupid and re-jected, but quickly recovered and re-approached Danny and said, "I know I was wrong, but I really want the job and know that I can play the shows well and I'll learn the tunes. Just give me a chance."

Since the job was the next day, Danny said, "O.K. The car leaves tomorrow at 52nd and Broadway at 1:00. Be there."

Harold was glad that Danny was willing to take a chance with him and hoped that everything would be all right.

Harold arrived at Kutcher's Saturday afternoon for the show's rehearsal and he felt that he had played his part well. That evening the band played for dancing before show time and the sub-leader (piano player) called a song that Harold wasn't sure of and he played some wrong notes. The leader had a fit and shouted at him, "If you don't know it, don't play it!"

Of course, he was right. Harold had wanted to do well, but he had goofed. After the show the leader called Danny and told him that Harold didn't know the business. The next day Danny made the two-hour trip from his house in New Jersey, and he also yelled at Harold, "I thought you knew the tunes, kid!"

Jay, the sax player, who liked Harold's playing, heard this conversation and asked Danny to give Harold another chance and he would help him learn the tunes. Danny, who later in his career became a close friend, said, "O.K., one more chance. If he doesn't learn the tunes by next Friday, I'll get someone else!" Every night Jay sat down with Harold back stage after everyone left and went over the important tunes for him to learn and memorize. Sometimes they didn't finish until 3:00 a.m. Harold learned the tunes and his club date reputation began to blossom.

As he became known as a trumpet player

who knew tunes, could fake harmonies, play strong "lead" for shows and could also improvise, Harold was able to make considerably more money as a result of out of town gigs that included extra pay for mileage and overtime (4 and 5 hour jobs became the norm). These bands worked on a "continuous" basis (50 minutes on, 10 minutes off), and more importantly the musicians were not required to stand while performing, (as Harold had to do in many catering halls) but instead would play while sitting on chairs for the duration of the job.

Fortunately, Harold met other sidemen who liked his playing and would remember him to other players and contractors. His first record date in N.Y.C. was obtained as a result of working with a club date bassist, the late Russ Saunders (Russ Savackus), who booked him for a jingle (TV/Radio commercial) featuring vocalist Page Morton singing the praises of "Chock Full of Nuts Coffee."

Perhaps Harold's biggest career boost came as a result of meeting and playing with drummer, "Mousey" Alexander. Besides being one of the truly great drummers, his personality was both friendly and extremely encouraging. He liked Harold (called him "Lieb") and became contractor for a talented and very busy jingle and record producer, George Roumanis. As a result, Harold was able to meet and play with the most successful and influential New York City musicians (Doc Severinsen, Bernie Glow, Ernie Royal, etc.), so his career was looking bright and promising.

In 1960, Harold played in the pit of the Broadway Show, "Vintage '60." It was fun, and although the show closed within two weeks, it gave Harold a chance to meet other musicians. He was also asked to play in "How to Succeed in Business," and "Purlie" but he declined, as he tired of playing the same notes over and over again each night.

To survive, before he could depend on a fairly stable income, Harold was a dishwasher, as well as an usher at the Plaza Theater on 56th Street where "Lust for Life" with Kirk Douglas and Anthony Quinn played during his entire six month tenure there. He was so bored as an usher that he would cut out the *Daily News* crossword puzzle, attach it to his flashlight with a rubber band and zone out. Unfortunately, or perhaps fortunately, he was fired when the theater manager discovered his transgression.

Meeting at a Concert

In 1959, on a cold night in February I had two tickets to a concert at the Juilliard School of Music on the upper West Side of New York City, where a piece by William Walton published by Oxford University Press was being performed. Since I couldn't find anyone to go with I turned in the extra ticket at the box office and went to my seat. I was reading the program notes when I became aware of someone stumbling over my knees to get to the seat next to me. I looked up to see a man with a head of dark wavy hair, wearing a three-piece suit and carrying a heavy overcoat and a trumpet case. I raised my eyebrows, no doubt exposing the blue eye shadow I sometimes wore and curled my lips in disbelief. It took a while for this person who obviously had bought the ticket I had turned in to settle down.

"Oh, look," my unexpected seat mate exclaimed, pointing to an entry in the program. "It says SPRING Quartet, instead of STRING Quartet."

I acknowledged this information with a grin and our eyes met.

"I had the craziest experience just before I came here," he rambled on. "I was teaching a kid in the Bronx and working on hitting high notes when he passed out on his bed. I called his mother to come into the room and she got hysterical! I didn't know what to do, but he recovered. I was really scared for a minute. That's never happened to me before!"

"Really! That's incredible!" I remarked.

Just then the concert mistress came out to cue the orchestra to tune, and the concert began. At the intermission, I quickly left my seat and mingled with the crowd, visited the ladies' room and waited for my new acquaintance to take his seat, avoiding him as long as possible.

The second half of the concert was as good as the first. After the applause died down, I began to stand up to put on my coat, when I heard a familiar voice.

"Would you like to get some tea?"

I looked at him and frowned, not knowing what to say.

"I just have to go upstairs and put my trumpet in my locker. I'll be right back."

I could have easily left the hall and never seen him again, but this was a sweet and music loving guy, and I was intrigued by his suggestion that I join him for tea instead of asking me to go with him to a sleazy bar. He seemed unthreatening and kind of funny. I was really attracted to the endearing quality he had of being comfortable enough to tell me (a total stranger) the bizarre experience he had with his student that afternoon.

My life was at a pretty low ebb. In September, I learned that my husband was in love with another woman. In March, I would be going to Mexico to get a divorce. What did I have to lose? I could spend some time with this friendly stranger in a public place and then take the bus down Broadway.

He saw me in the lobby when he came back from upstairs.

"I almost thought you wouldn't wait," he said. "The place I have in mind is across the street."

He took my arm as we pushed our way through the crowd moving toward the exit and he protectively steered me in the right direction as we crossed the busy street. We entered a Chinese Restaurant on the corner, where he motioned to an empty table and we sat down.

"You want some tea, right?"

"Sure," I said slipping off my coat.

"You want some soup or rice or something?" he asked

"No, I'm fine," I said.

"Two teas," he called to the waiter.

"So, you're a trumpet player?" I asked.

"Yeah, I'm finishing up my degree at Juilliard. I knew there was a trumpet piece on the program tonight, so I decided to go to the concert. My name's Harold, by the way. What's your name?" he asked. "What brought you out on such a cold night?"

"Oh, I love going to concerts!" I exclaimed. "My name's Toby," I said. "I work at Oxford University Press and get free tickets now and then. Actually, you obviously bought the ticket I turned in at the box office because I couldn't find anyone who wanted to go with me."

"No kidding, "he said, wide eyed "Well, I'll be." He had a nice smile and seemed very kind.

"You know," I said abruptly, "I should get home to feed my cat. He has a problem and I have to give him raw meat a few times a day - too much ash in the dry food. I'll just catch the next Broadway bus across the street."

"That's the bus I take too," he said. "Where do you live?"

"I'd rather not say," I said, putting on my coat and making my way to the door.

When we were on the bus I was flustered, and decided not to tell him my address or phone number, but then as I approached my stop I was afraid I might regret not seeing him again. I hurriedly scrawled my first name and my work number at Oxford University Press on a scrap of paper and told him to ask for the Music Department.

It took a couple of weeks for him to call me. He asked me to go to a movie and that was the beginning of our life together. In a classic case of serendipity, we had accidentally made a fortunate discovery, and as our relationship grew it was obvious that we were fated to be together. Exactly seven months and five days later we were married on September 18, 1959.

Getting to Know Each Other

Harold lived on 59th Street and 9th Ave. I lived on 73rd Street near Broadway. Before long we became lovers, and if he stayed overnight at my apartment we would walk down to Broadway for breakfast before I took the bus to work. Often, he would meet me for lunch at a deli around the corner from Oxford. We were getting to know each other, but I had not told him of my marital status. One day at lunch I said, "You know, there's something I want to tell you."

"A deep, dark secret?" He said with a grin.

"Well, I don't want it to be a secret, but I guess I would call it deep and dark," I said seriously.

"Tell," he urged.

"I just want you to know that I've been married for the last four years.

I met my husband in college in Indiana. We were both interested in acting and music, especially musical comedy. We began to discuss getting married after graduation and we both had a dream of going to New York City."

"I had the same dream." Harold said. "To be a trumpet player?" I asked.

"Yes," Harold said. "I lived in Hartford, Connecticut, and when I was seventeen I auditioned and was hired as the principal trumpet player in the Hartford Symphony. When Arthur Fiedler was guest conductor I was featured playing the "Trumpeter's Lullaby."

"So, I guess you were sort of a child prodigy!" I exclaimed.

"Well, I was going to the Hartt School of music. I had a good teacher and practiced a lot, and I thought I would try to get into the Symphony. But enough about me. Go on with your story," Harold urged.

"In 1957, we came to the City," I began. "I got a job at Oxford University Press and my husband got a job as a tour guide at NBC Studios until he decided to audition for a summer stock company in upstate, N.Y. I took the bus to see him every weekend. All the girls in the company were very nice to me except one, named Dottie. To make a long story short, they fell in love and I'm going to Mexico in March to get a divorce."

Harold looked at me tenderly and reached for my hand. "I'm sorry," he said.

I took his hand and told him that I was devastated at first but now I felt it was for the best because I wasn't sure we were ever really in love - that we were just good friends who helped each other get to New York.

As Harold walked me back to Oxford, he said, "I'll go to the airport with you in March and I'll meet you when you get back."

"Thanks," I said. "I could get to like you a lot!"

Harold called me after dinner and suggested that we take a walk up Broadway. He knew a great nut store where we could get a bag of pistachios to eat on the way. He picked me up and we began our walk, arm and arm.

"I can really understand how you feel about the break-up of your marriage. Even if you weren't in love, I'm sure it hurts."

"I was pretty hysterical at first, that's true," I said. "I'm still seeing a therapist."

"I recently broke off a relationship with a girl I was pretty crazy about," Harold said.

"What happened?" I asked

"We met when I was working in the Adirondacks doing a show. I had never felt like I was in love before. When the summer was over we both went back to the City. I was miserable and I wanted to keep seeing her. She lived in the Bronx and we agreed that if I wanted to see her there I should call first and we would meet at a certain coffee shop. Then we'd go to her apartment. She told me to always call first and not just go to her apartment, but one time I decided to go there anyway. When she opened the door I could see two little kids inside. She was furious!"

"Hey, this is the nut store. Let's get our pistachios." We went inside and were glad to warm up.

When we were outside again I said, "Let's find a coffee shop. I want to hear the rest of your story, but I'm really cold."

"Oh, sure, Harold said. "I know a place in this block."

We walked a short distance and went into a typical New York City 'no frills' coffee shop and found a booth.

"So finish your story," I said.

"Yeah, I was really shocked! I had no idea

she had kids. I was thinking I wanted to marry her, but I was in no position to support a family. I told my therapist, Dr. Berenda, and she convinced me that I needed to concentrate on my career. I had always thought I was stupid, but when I took tests that showed I had a decent I.Q., Dr. Berenda encouraged me to apply to Juilliard."

"So you did, and now you're almost through. And obviously, you seem to have gotten over that girl. I'm glad you told me about her."

"Yeah, but it was tough, and I really suffered for a while."

Harold told me that besides his therapy with Dr. Berenda and his correspondence with his trumpet teacher, Armando Ghitalla, the principal trumpet player with the Boston Symphony Orchestra, he kept grounded by listening to the New York Society of Ethical Culture Sunday morning radio broadcasts with their educational and humanistic lessons for life. (I began to listen with Harold and we sometimes attended the New York Society together. We especially enjoyed the musical interludes and were able to find musical works for trumpet and voice, which we performed there. Seeing our names appearing in the glass display case outside the building was a thrill for me!)

"We seem to have a lot in common," I said. "I'm thinking it can only get better."

"Me too," Harold agreed as we left the coffee shop. He opened the bag of nuts and we began to eat them, as we walked faster down Broadway against the wind. When we reached my apartment, it just seemed natural for Harold to spend the night. After a while we were sleeping in each other's apartment all the time.

One morning in March I reminded Harold that I would be going to Juarez, Mexico, in two weeks. I asked him if he still wanted to go with me to the airport.

"Of course, and just let me know when you're coming back, and I'll be there for you then too."

On March 18, we were on the subway early enough to have breakfast at JFK before I had to board. I felt butterflies in my stomach. I took Harold's hand and said, "I am so excited to get this over with, but I'm really nervous."

"Maybe you're just hungry?" Harold asked.

"Could be. Well, we'll be at JFK soon, and I'm so glad you're with me," I said squeezing Harold's hand.

"What a grip!" Harold squeezed back. "This girl is on her way!" We laughed.

Soon we were in a coffee shop at the airport and then it was time for me to go to the gate for El Paso, Texas, (just across the border from

Juarez). I took a big breath and looked into Harold's eyes. "I wish we were going on a trip together!"

"We will," Harold said, putting his arm around my waist.

It was time to board. Harold and I kissed and I was soon on my way to my aisle seat, straining to put my bag in the upper compartment. I sat down and closed my eyes, taking some deep yoga breaths until a girl excused herself and took the window seat. I hope she's not chatty, I thought. I want to relax and try to calm down.

My Divorce

I must have dozed for a time. When I came to, I was thinking how lucky I was that my husband, Dick, had found someone else, and in a few days, I would be free. Six months ago, when I first learned of his affair, I didn't see how I could go on, but now, especially since I met Harold, I felt that this was the best thing that could have happened. Actually, Dick and I were really good friends but our sex life was superficial and lacking in passion.

My reverie was interrupted by the arrival of the snack cart at my seat. I was jarred back to the reality that I would soon be in El Paso, and the butterflies returned, reminding me of the mission that would really change my life.

When I left the airport, I took a cab to my hotel in El Paso. My room was artless and stark, just supplied with the basics, but I felt like a princess in a castle. I was so excited and happy to be on my own!

I went to the restaurant in the hotel and had a light meal. Back in my room I watched some T.V., read for a while, danced around watching my reflection in the mirror, posing like a diva. I was totally exuberant! I pulled back the covers, doused the lights, jumped into bed, thought of Harold and closed my eyes.

The next day I took a cab across the border to Juarez, Mexico, to keep my appointment with the lawyer who was to represent me in court. He had already received the paper work from my New York lawyer.

"Mrs. Turmail?" he asked, offering me his hand. "I am Juan Hernandez. I'll be representing you in the court."

"Yes, I am Mrs. Turmail. I'm so glad to meet you!" I said, shaking his hand.

Mr. Hernandez was smartly dressed in a dark blue pin striped suit with a white shirt and dark purple tie. His black hair was cut to just above the ears and slicked smoothly away from his forehead, no doubt with the help of some kind of pomade. He had a dark complexion and brown eyes behind brown square framed glasses. His pleasant smile and hearty handshake put me at ease. I felt quite comfortable with him and immediately felt that he could be trusted to be a complete professional.

"You are free to go now. Just come back in an hour and you will have your divorce. All the documents will be sent to your New York lawyer who will give you and Mr. Turmail the official divorce papers."

"Thank you," I said. "I guess I'll take a walk." I left the office and soon saw a short distance away what reminded me of a flea market. I decided to explore the area until it was time to return to the law office. The people going about their business seemed to stare at me, but as an American woman I was obviously out of place, so it was to be expected that they would be curious.

When I went back to the law office, Mr. Hernandez was seated at his desk. He stood and again we shook hands.

"Is it all over?" I asked.

"You are officially divorced," Mr. Hernandez assured me. "As I told you, your New York lawyer will give you the divorce papers."

"Thank you so much! I can't believe how quickly it all went. Would you be able to get me a cab to take me back to El Paso?"

"Of course," Mr. Hernandez said, making the call. "Yes," he smiled. "I understand that the Americans call these Mexican divorces 'quickie divorces.'"

"Now I see why!" I laughed. "Goodbye now," I said opening the door to the street.

"Goodbye to you and good luck," Mr. Hernandez said.

I sat on a bench outside the office until the cab came. I was ecstatic as I was whisked back to El Paso. My bag was packed and within the hour I took another cab to the airport in time to catch my plane back to New York.

Moving In Together

On the return trip I was relaxed and relieved. I thought about Harold and our future together. I couldn't wait to see him at the airport
where he was to meet my flight. Though we had
met only a month ago, we had easily fallen into
a close relationship. I hoped it wasn't because I
was needy and he was kind, but I had grown at-
tached to him. I just didn't want to make another
choice I might regret. We would need to take it
slowly and I would be wise to notice any red
flags along the way. In the meantime, I knew I
wanted to be with him and I believed he felt the
same way. I think that perhaps when you've been
in a loveless marriage you know when you are
experiencing real love, especially when it includes passion, not just a weak facsimile.

When the plane landed, I rushed along the
corridor to the gate and into Harold's arms.

"I'm a divorcee," I giggled. "Do you still love me?" I asked coyly.

"Did I say I love you?" Harold said, giving me a big kiss.

"Say it now," I said with a laugh.

"I love you," Harold said close to my ear.

"Hungry?"

"Famished!"

We went into a small Italian place with red checkered table cloths where the waiter put us at a table near the front window. We ordered wine.

"Your first meal with me as a single girl," I said fluttering my eyelashes flirtatiously and reaching for his hand.

Harold took my other hand and looked into my eyes with an intensity that I hadn't noticed before. I felt my heart racing.

We agreed that Harold would get a friend

with a car to help him move my things to his apartment, which was bigger than mine and had a tub and shower in the kitchen with a metal cover to use when preparing meals.

The first night that the 59th Street apartment was officially our home, Harold said, "Pretty fancy, huh?"

"Yeah," I sighed, shrugging my shoulders, tilting my head and grinning in mock shyness. "I'm moving up, right?"

(My apartment was on the second floor. Harold lived in a fifth floor walk up.)

We were very much in love and quite happy living together in Harold's apartment on 59th Street and 10th Ave. for $27.00 a month (toilet down the hall). Harold told me that he loved this apartment. It was like a palace to him. He loved the neighborhood and the energy he felt. Living here was a totally new and exhilarating experience, compared to his life in suburban

Hartford.

I loved it too, but then I loved everything about New York!

Our personal routines didn't change, but it was so comforting to be in one apartment. I was still working at Oxford University Press. I took a voice lesson once a week, sang in the chorus of a small opera company and had a church job in lower Manhattan singing in the choir, where I became good friends with two of the women. Harold went to the Union Floor at Roseland Ballroom three days a week to book his club date gigs.

Harold looked so handsome in his tux. I thought of him as a soldier in his uniform going to battle. He had told me that no matter how often he did a club date he became anxious - not about playing the trumpet, but hoping he wouldn't be late, or if he had to get there by sub-way worrying that he might get mugged at three o'clock in the morning.

When he was working late I always tried to stay up until he came home, but I often drifted off to sleep reading a book, feeling cared for and secure. I had so much respect for him. He was kind and good and dedicated to his goals, and now he was also dedicated to me.

Listening to him practice I was deeply touched by his beautiful, lyrical tone. I couldn't wait to hear him play baroque music soon with a brass group in an evening church concert.

Brass Quintet Concert

I had been to many church concerts, but this one was special because it was the first time I would hear Harold play classical music with a brass quintet. I was seated in the front row of a beautiful episcopal church in the sixties near Broadway. Organ music created an ambient air of serenity. People continued to trickle in, while others were seated, some looking at their programs listing works by Thomas Tallis, Josquin Des Prez, William Byrd and Claudio Monte-Verdi.

Surrounded by stained glass windows and colorful bouquets of flowers on either side of the altar, I experienced a feeling of peace and contentment as my eyes were led to the vaulted ceiling above. Nevertheless, I felt an inner nervous excitement as I anticipated hearing Harold play.

The organ stopped. The group of five musicians dressed in tuxes (two trumpets, a trombone, a French horn and a tuba) came through a door and sat on folding chairs placed in front of the altar. They put their music on individual music stands, and the concert began.

The rich sonorous sound of the ensemble enhanced by the acoustics of the church was startling at first but utterly glorious! As each work was performed I strained to pick out Harold's tone, and, if for a moment he played alone, I was thrilled by his lyrical sound. How can I be so lucky, I wondered, to be connected to this man and to be able to hear him play my favorite kind of music. Maybe there are works for soprano and trumpet that we could do together! What a thought!

As the concert ended, the organ began a spirited piece and the people began to file out. The soloists returned to the anteroom and I waited in the foyer of the church for Harold to join me. When he appeared, I threw my arms around him!

"This was totally invigorating!" I gushed. "You were amazing! Your tone is so beautiful! I know I can't go to all your jobs but I want to hear you play as often as I can!"

"I'll try to remember that," Harold said, laughing. "I was that good, huh?" he said with a grin. "I'm kinda tired," he said. Wanna go home?"

"Sure," I said. "Can I take a nap with you?"

"We'll see," he joked, taking my arm as we went to the subway.

Marry a Musician?

Winter was finally over and the weather was warm enough for us to go to Bryant Park on my lunch hour at Oxford and eat a bag lunch. One day in May on my birthday Harold brought me a bouquet of flowers.

"Happy Birthday," Harold said, giving me a kiss.

"You sweetheart!" I cried. "Thank you! Will a ring be next?" I teased.

I told him we could just go to City Hall with a witness or two and make it official.

Harold said he had a friend, Willard Bond, who worked in a resort in the Adirondacks in the summer, and maybe his wife, Brenda, and he would be our witnesses in the fall.

I was so excited! I grabbed Harold's arm, snatched my flowers, and began to rush across the grass to get back to Oxford.

"Hey, I have to get back to work! We're going to get married," I shouted. "We're going to get married!" Some people looked up and smiled or gave us "thumbs up."

We hugged goodbye.

"See you tonight," I said hurriedly. "I'll be there!" Harold said.

September 19, 1959, I put on a simple navy blue dress with matching jacket that I often wore to work with low heeled navy blue pumps and Harold wore the suit he wore the night we met. We took a subway to City Hall and waited outside for Willard and Brenda. When they arrived, we went to the room where marriages were performed. The door was closed and a few couples with their witnesses were sitting on benches outside. We found a place and sat down, making small talk for what seemed an endless time until it was our turn.

We entered a small room set up with folding chairs and a podium on one side where an official seemed ready to perform the next ceremony. He was a middle-aged man with graying black straight hair showing a receding hair line, who wore a slightly rumpled grey suit, polished black wingtip shoes and a bright abstract design multi colored tie which gave his ensemble a dashing touch of celebration. He smiled at us and beckoned to us to approach the podium. Harold handed him our papers which he quickly scanned and said, looking at Harold,

"You are Harold Lieberman?"

"Yes sir," Harold replied.

"And who is Miss Gershon?" he asked.

I stood next to Harold and said, "I am."

"And these are your witnesses?" he asked, glancing at Willard and Brenda.

"We are," they said.

"My name is Edward McCarthy," he said. "By the powers invested in me by the state of New York, I'll be conducting this ceremony. Well, we'll get started then," he began.

I don't remember the first part of his remarks, but when he asked, looking at Harold, "Do you accept Toby in all anniversary?"

I uttered a giggle and thought, I guess he means adversity.

Harold replied, trying to suppress a laugh, "I do."

And when it was my turn to answer the same question, I said, "I do," trying not to laugh out loud.

We could hear Willard and Brenda whispering.

"I now pronounce you man and wife. You may kiss the bride."

Harold and I tried to regain our composure, looked intently into each other's eyes and kissed lingeringly. We all shook Mr. McCarthy's hand, and Harold and I signed a paper that he had signed making our marriage official.

We jovially left City Hall and took a subway to Willard and Brenda's loft on the lower East Side. Willard was an artist. He was tall and lanky and had shoulder length black hair. He wore a black suit and red polka dot tie with a red silk handkerchief poking out of his breast pocket. Brenda had long straight brown hair with straight bangs. She was medium height and her little black dress showed her trim figure. Around her neck, she wore a lavender and red silk scarf that was creatively knotted and flowed to her waist.

I was fascinated by the arrangement of the living space. There were definite areas for sleeping, cooking, eating and one for entertaining with couches and chairs, and, of course, a huge area devoted to Willard's art projects of painting and creating large pieces fusing metal and glass. Brenda had her own corner of the loft where she did her work of illustrating children's books.

Champagne and cake was eventually set out on the table. The cork was popped and our glasses filled.

"Congratulations!" Willard exclaimed, raising his glass in a toast. "All the best!"

"Yes!" Brenda added, as we all clinked our glasses.

"This is very nice, by the way," Harold responded. "Thanks!"

"Of course, man!" Willard gave Harold a bear hug.

"Thanks so much for being our best couple!" I said, hugging them both.

"You know," Harold mumbled, "this

probably sounds crazy, my wedding day and all, but I have to get home and practice."

"Honestly, Honey? Today?" I asked incredulously.

"I know." Harold looked a little embarrassed. "But I've got an important gig tomorrow, and I have to keep up my lip."

I understood, of course, but for a moment I thought, "What have I done?" But I never looked back and the more I heard Harold play the more I supported him in every way. He was so gifted and had such a beautiful tone when he played that I wanted him to perform wherever and whenever he could; and to do that he had to practice every day.

Smiths

After his success with Danny Lapedus at Kutcher's resort, Harold was able to count on getting more jobs in the Catskills.

In 1957, on one of those jobs he met Derek Smith, an excellent jazz pianist, (and his wife Shirley), who had left their native England, hoping that Derek could build a career in the music business in New York City. To eke out a living they found jobs at Macy's. Shirley became a sales lady, and Derek sat at a grand piano on the first floor and played the tunes of the day.

Derek's next step was similar to Harold's. He got gigs by going to the Union Floor and began working his way up doing club dates and playing in the mountains.

Although we lived in different locations we managed to get together as much as possible.

Through the years, we made tennis dates at out-door courts (when our daughter was under a year old we put her in a play pen outside the fence), as well as traveling to each other's homes for lunch or dinner.

I remember one time when Derek and Harold had a gig at a venue for a group of apartment residents called the "Cliff Dwellers." Shirley and I couldn't really talk much, surrounded as we were by the din of the music and the merriment of the dancers. In fact, I began to feel like a "wallflower" until one of the young men approached me and asked me to dance. That made my day!

We and the Smiths eventually moved to the same town and became best friends.

During his career, Derek became the piano player on the NBC "Tonight Show" until it moved to the West Coast (Derek and Shirley chose to stay in New York). He often played concerts with Dick Hymen (a very successful jazz piano player), and also did a one man show, led a band on a T.V. show called "Musical Chairs," made many records and radio and T.V. commercials and was the piano player in some of Woody Allen's movies, until Woody wanted him to change his hairstyle for one. Derek was always 'his own person,' and that was something he didn't care to do.

In 2014, Derek was diagnosed with cancer and after a determined and courageous two-year struggle (with Shirley by his side), he passed away shortly before his 85th birthday.

Derek was an energetic and passionate jazz piano player, but most of all he was a happy man — a family man with a big heart, a charming smile and a marvelous laugh. We will always feel his loss, but in a way, we feel he is still with us.

Getting A Master's Degree

Even though Harold had now achieved some success as a versatile New York City trumpet player, he decided to take the suggestion of Tommy Newsome, a buddy he had met in the Air Force, to get a master's degree at Columbia University, as Tommy had done. "You never know when you might need it in case you can't blow your horn," Tommy had advised him. Harold applied and enrolled, easily completing the work in a year.

While he was taking classes, he told me there was an elementary school on the campus for students' observation in that field. I wanted to leave my job at Oxford and I thought I might get some ideas about teaching if I visited the school. After sitting in on various classes I realized that the youngest children were the most interesting to me, and if I did decide to be a teacher, I would choose the area of Early Childhood.

One morning when we took the subway to Columbia, as we walked to the campus, I said, "You know, I'm getting really confused."

"Why?" Harold asked. "What's wrong?"

"Nothing, really, I said. "I've just been thinking that I'd like to go back to school to get certified in the field of Early Childhood, but I'm 28 years old, and if we're going to start a family I think this is the time. What do you think?"

"We can't really discuss it right now, but I'll do whatever you want," Harold said, giving me a quick kiss and racing to his class.

So, I decided right then and there. I wanted to try for a baby!

When I became pregnant within months, we were amazed and found a doctor through the Musician's Union, who was affiliated with

Flower Fifth Avenue Hospital. We signed up for prenatal classes where we prepared for natural childbirth.

As my pregnancy progressed, we realized we would need to move from our small fifth floor walkup, and knowing we couldn't afford a bigger New York apartment we started a search in Westchester County. We decided on Mt. Vernon, New York, the first train stop in Westchester from New York City. We were sorry to leave the City, but the grass and trees with a park within walking distance was a bonus.

Now that Harold had teaching credentials, and with the impending birth of a baby, he sent letters to various schools in the Westchester area. The Supervisor of Music in New Rochelle, N.Y., responded and told Harold that a high school instrumental music teacher had just been fired and he needed a replacement for the remainder of the year. He asked Harold to come in the next day for an interview and gave him the directions to the high school.

After Mr. Sawyer introduced himself he looked over Harold's credentials and found them satisfactory. He said he had interviewed several applicants and was eager to find the right person to take over, as a substitute teacher had been in charge for two weeks and the band was in limbo as a result. He explained the salary level and urged Harold to consider accepting the offer and begin the next day.

If nothing else, Harold saw this position as an easy way to add to his income. He shook Mr. Sawyer's outstretched hand enthusiastically, and said, "O.K., I'll do it."

When he entered the band room the next day, Mr. Sawyer introduced Harold as a permanent teacher for the rest of the year. As soon as Harold was alone with the students, there were definitely some challenges. Not only was there talking and laughing amongst the group, but Harold was startled when he saw a drum stick flying through the air, which became stuck in the acoustic ceiling.

Harold's class work at Columbia had not prepared him for class management and he angrily shouted, "Stop! You don't throw a drumstick at the ceiling. I'll have to report you to Mr. Sawyer!" which simply elicited louder talking and laughter. For better or for worse, the band was now in Harold's (sweaty) hands.

Harold's biggest personal challenge was to organize this marching band's performance at the annual Thanksgiving football game between Iona High and New Rochelle. During the half, the band traditionally marched to the center of the field and while facing the Iona side, formed an "I." After playing another march, the band turned around and would form an "N & R." This was definitely not covered in any course work

Harold had taken at any school, and he was totally preoccupied with his lack of experience to carry out such a task.

"Tobe," he said, "will you come with me to the field? I'm at a complete loss! I don't have a clue! What did I get myself into?"

"You're so silly!" I couldn't stop laughing. "It's a good thing I'm used to your sense of humor! When you get to that field, you're on your own, baby!"

"You know what?" Harold exclaimed. "I'll just instruct the kids that when I blow one whistle, they should somehow form an "I"; two whistles, an "N" & "R.""

"Then, "I cackled, "the next Monday you'll get fired!"

"If I don't, I'll simply quit. Maybe my master's degree will come in handy someday, but for now my music gigs will have to do!"

"Right," I laughed uncontrollably.

Toots Thielemans - Benny's Visit

When Harold and I lived in Mt. Vernon, N.Y., we first met Toots Thielemans, a world-famous jazz harmonica player, whistler and guitarist, and his wife, Trinetta in a Yonkers restaurant nearby. Harold was aware that Toots performed regularly on the children's T.V. program, "Sesame Street," but more impressive to Harold was Toot's reputation as one of the best jazz musicians in the world. Harold was thrilled to meet him![2]

On the way home Harold told me that Toots and Trinetta were born in Belgium and now lived in Yonkers. Since Toots didn't drive, Harold offered to drive him to the Union Floor three days a week. Toots was working on composing a new song, which became "Bluesette," a

---

[2] Larry Adler was an equally famous harmonica player, but he was known for his artistry in performing transcriptions of the classics, such as violin concertos by Bach and Vivaldi, as well as making albums with pop stars like Elton John, Elvis and Cher, and writing film scores.

major hit, and Harold was witness to its evolution, as he and Toots drove to and from Manhattan week after week.

Toots was on the Jimmy Dean T.V. show where he sometimes needed to read music, which wasn't his forte. Harold was able to give him some tips where needed. They developed a real mutual respect and friendship.

During that time, one day our buzzer rang and when Harold answered it and asked who was there, he was stunned to hear a soft voice say, "Your brother, Benny."

Harold shouted into the intercom, "How did you know where to find me? Come on up!"

A few minutes later our bell rang. When Harold opened the door, we saw an emaciated man with a very serious look on his face.

"Come in! Come in," Harold urged, as

he hugged his brother who was holding a shopping bag. "This is my wife, Toby, Benny. Sit down. I'll take your bag."

"Benny, I'm so glad to meet you!" I said. "Please sit down."

Benny sat down, but kept his bag by his side. Still not smiling, Benny reached into the bag and took out a box. "I've been selling these," he explained. "I want you to have this one. Open the box."

Harold opened the box and took out a very cheap looking ceramic object of two Asian looking figures on a thin wooden platform - an item that people sometimes put on top of a T.V. or on a shelf.

I looked at Harold quizzically and said, "Thanks, Benny."

"Yes," echoed Harold. "Thanks! We'll put it right here," he said, placing it on the T.V.

Benny reached into the bag and said, his expression never changing, "You don't call your mother. You should call your mother. I brought this recording machine. I want you to say something to your mother."

"I'm sorry, Benny," Harold replied. "I have nothing to say to her."

"You should talk to your mother," Benny repeated, becoming agitated.

Harold told Benny he had to drive into Manhattan to the Musician's Union to book some jobs and he was going to pick up Toots Thielemans, the jazz musician on the way.

Benny looked confused, but Harold took his arm, grabbed their coats and headed for the door.

When they came back Benny looked uncomfortable and nervous. "I have to go," he said. He put the wire recording device in his bag and rushed to the door.

"Benny, man, stay for a while," Harold coaxed. "Toby made a nice dinner."

"I have to go," Benny said again and opened the apartment door.

Harold and I went to the door, but before we could say goodbye Benny ran to the elevator, not turning back.

Harold was shaken and with tears in his eyes he said sadly, "I never should have taken him to the Union. Listening to Toots playing the harmonica in the car was a negative experience. I think it just stirred up the regrets he has about his life. He's very disturbed. It was overwhelming to him.

He was never the same after the war. He was in the Panther Division and fought in the Battle of the Bulge. He was such a talented clarinet player (sounded just like Benny Goodman), so sensitive and smart. I guess his battle experiences pretty much destroyed him."

We never saw him again.

Benny Goodman

In 1962, Benny Goodman and the band returned from their tour of Russia. Harold's dear friend, Tommy Newsome (who was at that time writing arrangements and conducting on NBC's "The Tonight Show," along with the trumpet player, Doc Severinsen) called.

"Hey, Lieb," Tommy said, "Benny's auditioning guys to tour the United States. I think it would be a great move for you. Auditions are tomorrow at the Ansonia Hotel on 73rd Street and Broadway. Just show up, meet me in the lobby, and I'll clue you in from there."

"Wow! Harold exclaimed. "Thanks, man! Of course, I'll be there! See you tomorrow."

As a kid, Harold idolized Benny Goodman and his phenomenal jazz improvisational ability. To audition for him was not only exciting, but a chance of a lifetime.

When he met Tommy the next day,
Tommy said, "If Benny likes you, he'll tell the
guys to take a break and his agent, Jay, will approach you and ask you your price. Say, $475.00
a week."

"Tommy, I can't believe what you're telling me! I'll go for a $100.00 a week."

"No, no, man!" Tommy declared. "That's
not the way to do it. Trust me! Just do what I'm
telling you! Now let's go upstairs. You'll do
great!"

"O.K., O.K.," Harold said. "I'll do my best!
Whatever you say!"

The "King," as the guys referred to him,
took an hour before he found a suitable reed for
his clarinet and eventually he called out a number that, luckily, Harold was familiar with, "The
Angels Sing," (a hit for Benny's trumpeter,
Ziggy Elman in the 40's.) After Harold played

the solo, the guys in the band turned around and gave him signs of "well done."

"Take a break, guys," Benny said, as Tommy had predicted.

Harold saw Jay approaching him, and he said, "What's your price?"

Harold replied, "$475.00 per week."

Jay said, "I'll be right back," and then he went over to Benny and came back to Harold, saying, "Benny will go as high as $450.00 per week."

Thrilled, and with a throbbing heart, Harold replied as cooly as possible, "O.K., I'll take it."

The tour through the United States ended in "Freedomland" in the Bronx (now, Co-op City.) I was able to be there, and Harold intro-duced me to Benny. It was very exciting to see my man on the stage with The King, and I couldn't wait to hear him play with the band. When the performance was over, I waited patiently for Harold to leave the bandstand, so I could give him a big hug.

When we embraced, I noticed that he looked perturbed. "What's wrong?" I asked. "I'm so proud of you! What a thrill!"

"You know," Harold said, "Benny knew you were in the audience. He often gives me a solo, even if it's a short one, and it's almost as if he didn't give me one because you were here."

"Oh, Honey," I said. "Don't feel bad! I feel wonderful! Maybe a big band leader like Benny just doesn't think in those terms. Just think, you've played with one of the greats! That's what counts!" I took Harold's hand, and we went to our car.

On the way home Harold needed to do some more processing about Benny.

"Don't get me wrong," he said. "Playing with Benny will always be one of the highlights of my life, but he is difficult to play for, as you never know if he really likes you or might fire you. One evening at Chicago's Ravinia Music Festival, Benny called out, "The Angels Sing," and after my performance, which I thought was o.k., he came over to me on stage in front of several thousand people and said, 'Hey, pops, (everyone was called 'pops'), you sound too Jewish. Trade your part with Cootie.' (Cootie Williams of Duke Ellington fame.) I couldn't believe that he would say this to me, as the song is a Jewish Freilach performed at weddings and Bar/Bat Mitzvahs, and I thought that I was indeed capturing the style. The next night, Cootie (a great stylist, but poor reader) struggled with the part, and I felt sorry for him, as it was not, "his bag." Again, Benny came over to me with his planted half-smile and said, 'Hey, pops, that's the way you should play it.' "

"I see what you mean, Honey," I said. "It's like walking on eggs. But you know what?" I added, trying to cheer him up with a worn-out cliche, "You've got a lot more fish to fry!"

"Whoa," Harold laughed. "I guess I got carried away! Let's take a break at the next diner."

"Good idea," I agreed. "Then we can get home to the sitter and put our little Rhonda girl to bed. I think she missed you while you were away."

Leaving Mt. Vernon

In 1964, when Rhonda was three years old we needed a larger apartment. On one of their rides into Manhattan, Toots told Harold that there was an apartment available in a high rise building next to his. When we looked at it, with its larger rooms, a terrace, a pool, a view of the Hudson River and convenient train service into Manhattan, we eagerly took over a one year lease.

One of the couples we met were Ted and Angela Cooper and their three-year-old son, who became a playmate for Rhonda. Ted was an English teacher in Manhattan, as well as an A&R (Artists and Repertoire) man for Epic Records. As Ted and Harold got to know each other, Ted hired Harold as a contractor for some of his record projects. As a contractor, Harold made contacts with many musicians, (including a violinist named Irving Spice, who got other violinists if they were needed. Irving was quite a character and behind his back Ted and Harold dubbed him "Irving Spice and his Mice"). Harold was hired by other record contractors as a trumpet player, building up his reputation as a studio musician and increasing his income. (Years later we learned that Ted and Angela divorced and Ted remarried, bought a house in Westchester and one day committed suicide by jumping out a window - which his father had done before him.).

Meanwhile, I was eager to begin my work on getting certification to teach in the field of early childhood. I enrolled at Hunter College in Manhattan and was able to go at night, hiring baby sitters if Harold had gigs.

When there was a suicide on our floor and we became aware there was a swingers sex club in our building, we felt disenchanted with our location.

We were fortunate that we had signed only

a one year lease and were glad to leave the roaches and paper-thin walls (announcing each toilet flush from adjoining apartments). We were ready to look for a house. After working with real estate brokers in Westchester County and sensing that we couldn't afford to live there, we decided to cross the George Washington Bridge to New Jersey and try our luck in Englewood, a town with a mixed black and white population. This was, after all, the 1960's, when integration of the public schools was a big issue and we wanted to be part of the solution.

We found an affordable two story, colonial house in Englewood, described in the *New York Times* as "Cute and Cozy," not far from an entrance to a highway leading to the George Washington Bridge, making it easy for Harold to get into Manhattan for record dates and jingles (radio and T.V. ads) that not only increased his income, but also paid residuals each time the ad was aired.

An elementary school, as well as a bus stop going into Manhattan, were within walking distance. We were very happy in Englewood where our son, Aaron, was born in 1967. By that time I had completed my courses at Hunter College and was now certified to teach pre-school through second grade.

I had read Betty Friedan's book, "The Feminine Mystique," which discussed the plight of some housewives of the 50's, who were beginning to feel unfulfilled in their traditional role of wife and mother and wanted to use their education to get recognition outside of the home. These ideas resonated with me and gave me confidence to consider looking for a teaching job. After sending my resumé to several preschools in the area, I interviewed at a few and was hired to teach a morning class of three year olds at a small school nearby. I looked forward to this change in my life, but I was apprehensive about the need to hire a caregiver for Aaron, who was only eighteen months old. Nevertheless, I bravely put an ad in the local paper and eventually hired a young black woman who had a child of her own. I wondered how she felt having to leave her child to care for mine, but I didn't feel it was my business to ask. She was cheerful and easy to talk to, and I was excited to go to work every morning. I enjoyed planning for and working with my class, and socializing with the other teachers.

One day when I got home and went into the kitchen I saw Aaron in his highchair across from Jasmine, the care giver, with her head leaning on her right hand, with her eyes closed. There was no interaction between them. Aaron wriggled in his chair and made some whining sounds. I went to him and picked him up, putting him on my lap, as I stared at Jasmine who had not changed her position.

Was she thinking about her child? I wondered. Was I just projecting my concern about leaving my baby with anyone at all? Did I hire this girl because she was black and I wanted to believe that was the thing to do? Was I showing prejudice because deep down I was wondering if she wasn't relating to Aaron because she was black? I was very confused.

Betty Friedan hadn't written a chapter on how new mothers might react to their feelings of conflict with their frustration in traditional roles in the home and their personal natural maternal instincts. I wasn't ready to do this, I thought. I had to choose my baby over my work. Maybe when Aaron was older I could try again.

I put my hand on Jasmine's shoulder and she lifted her head.

"Jasmine," I asked. "Are you tired?"

"Oh, no, Miss Toby, I'm fine," she said, shaking her head and looking around.

"Jasmine," I said. "I can't do this. I miss my baby too much. I won't need you any more. I hope you understand."

"Oh, Miss Toby," Jasmine exclaimed standing up. "I like your baby. I won't do this again."

"I'm sorry," I told her. "Jasmine, who takes care of your child when you work?"

"Oh, my Mom, Miss Toby. I gotta work!"

"You're very fortunate to have your Mom, Jasmine. I'm glad she's with your child. I really like you, and I'm glad we met."

"I'm glad we met too, Miss Toby."

"Will you hold Aaron while I get my purse?" I asked. "I want to pay you for this week."

Jasmine took Aaron in her arms and looked forlorn.

I wrote a check to cash and put it on the

table, as I took Aaron from her and put him in his bouncy chair.

"Thank you, Miss Toby."

We walked to the front door. I put my arms around her, tears in my eyes.

She responded with a hug.

"Thank you, Jasmine. Good luck to you!" I opened the door. She was crying too and quickly left the house.

By the time Aaron was four years old we were delighted to send him to an integrated public pre-school in Englewood. Rhonda, however, experienced some frustration in the fourth grade when she was separated from her best friend on a field trip because her teacher, Mrs. Battle, (who was black) paired each white child with a black child. We tried to explain the teacher's wish to help children from different neighborhoods get to know each other. She and her friend, Marla would have many other times to be together. We did become concerned when Rhonda came home one day and told us that when she was the last one to enter the classroom after recess Mrs. Battle scolded her and shook her by the shoulders. We discussed the matter with the guidance counselor. He suggested that Rhonda, Harold, Mrs. Battle and I meet with him and discuss what happened.

This encounter, in retrospect, was the beginning of our daughter's ability to advocate for herself. We were very proud of her for her ability to confront Mrs. Battle and to express how she felt afraid and ashamed by the experience. Mrs. Battle had little to say in her own defense, but the meeting did end amicably. We had chosen Englewood to be part of the integration solution. These two incidents made us realize that it might not be easy.

The 1960's was a tumultuous time in our

country. Harold and I were focused on our personal lives, working, going to school and raising our children, and we were only peripherally attuned to world events, but we were aware of Dr. Martin Luther King's movement of civil disobedience and the rise of other factions desiring more extreme measures to speak to the needs of the black population's demands for justice and recognition. We had heard of "Black Power" and "Black is Beautiful," and we had heard of random black groups rioting in various states. And then we heard of blacks rioting in our town of Englewood. We were not personally impacted by those riots, because although the schools were now integrated, the neighborhoods were not.

In Englewood, there were four wards: the first ward was populated by the wealthy, who in the early settling of the town needed servants to keep up their properties. The workers needed

housing of their own and settled in the down-
town district, which was now the fourth ward.
The second ward, where we lived, was middle
class and near the George Washington Bridge;
and the third ward, beyond the business district,
was also middle class and slowly becoming integrated.

As we became more aware of the country's turmoil and the need for integration, our
consciousness was raised, and when a black man
decided to run for mayor we asked our neighbors
to come to a "coffee" to meet him and discuss
issues that needed to be addressed in Englewood. We were trying to make a difference.

We stayed in Englewood for eight years
until Rhonda was twelve and Aaron was six. By
that time Harold was teaching music courses at
Ramapo College, and because he ran a summer
jazz festival and played both day and night time
concerts, we had been wondering if we should

move closer to the campus. But, I think even more of a concern was our experience in Englewood. By the time Rhonda finished elementary school, her good friends had either moved or were going to private schools. Although she was getting good grades, when I looked at her work I found it really didn't merit more than "C"s. The classes were integrated, but the only black girl we met personally was one Rhonda asked to a birthday party. The kids didn't live near each other, and they really didn't integrate socially. Yes, we wanted to be "part of the solution," but we wanted to be sure our children had friends and were getting the best education they could. We decided to move to the town of Ridgewood, which was closer to Ramapo and had a good reputation for academics and music.

I cried when we left Englewood. I liked living there and I felt sad that we had to admit that for our children's needs, it had fallen short.

My Very First Band
Age 15
"The Rhythm Kings"
1946

CABARET AND PUBLIC DANCE HALL
EMPLOYEE'S IDENTIFICATION CARD
Division of Licenses, 156 Greenwich St., N.Y. 6, N.Y.
(RIGHT THUMB PRINT)

ISSUED BY

No. 618471 DATE ISSUED SEP 8 1957

NAME Harold J. Lieberman

ASSUMED NAME

OCCUPATION Musician

AGE 26 HEIGHT 5 FT. 8 IN. WEIGHT 160 LBS. MALE

HAIR Brown EYES Blue

EXPIRES AUGUST 31, 1959

Carnegie Recital

July 1978 - Woody Herman - Rhonda Joy -Toby - Harold

Jazz Impact

Aaron performing

The Donald

In 1985, Harold was playing a gig at the Waldorf Hotel when a tall well-built man in a tuxedo walked on stage and began talking to Lester Lanin, the band leader. Lester called the tune, "New York, New York," and the tall man grabbed the microphone from its stand and began to belt out, in and out of tune:

"Start spreading the News,

I'm leaving today,

I want to be part of it,

New York, New York," etc., etc.

"I wanna wake up in a city that doesn't sleep.

And find I'm king of the hill."

(motioning to the band to play louder), singing louder and louder: "top of the heap!"

Wildly waving his free hand in the air.

Returning the mike to its stand, he stood close to it and both arms conducting, finished with a flourish:

"And if I can make it there - I'll make it anywhere, come on, come true - New York, New York!"

As he walked off the stage grinning, with both arms up in the air, hands clasped like a triumphant prize fighter, the band members turned to one another in disbelief.

"Who is this guy?" several of them asked.

Lester was laughing and patted the man on the back.

"That's Donald Trump, fellas," he said clapping.

Harold had never heard of him, but by 2016, he was running for president of the United States and getting enough votes in the primaries to be considered the presumptive nominee of the

Republican Party.

With no political experience and a completely unorthodox style of campaigning, Trump's message to "Make America Great Again," won him enough electoral votes in the general election to become President of the United States!

Harold witnessed Trump's dauntless demeanor first hand and has included the incident in his collection of memorable anecdotes.

Ethical Culture in New Jersey

When we moved to Englewood, New Jersey, we learned that there was a Society for Ethical Culture in the nearby town of Teaneck. In 1966, when our daughter, Rhonda, was five years old we enrolled her in the Sunday school and began to attend the Sunday morning meetings where we made many friends and often performed together or alone during the musical interlude.

One couple we met were Virginia Wexelblat, who was a beautiful tall brunette who sang in the Metropolitan Opera chorus and her husband, Herb, who played tuba in the Met orchestra. Virginia was in charge of programming the music for Sunday services and appreciated our talent. She encouraged Harold to perform an entire evening recital at the meeting house, but at first Harold rejected the idea because he felt he would be too nervous in front of a live, intimate group. When he graduated from Juilliard, he had a choice to play for a jury or give a recital, and he chose a jury, feeling it would be less stressful. Virginia was very persistent, and with my encouragement he decided to meet the challenge, preparing a program of classical pieces.

The assembled audience filled the room. Familiar faces were there including our next-door neighbors, Loren Glickman,[3] first bassoon player with the Mostly Mozart Concerts at Lincoln Center, and his wife, Dobbie, a respected piano teacher. Soon Harold and his accompanist, Fran Honig, a former child prodigy, entered the room to an enthusiastic round of applause.

Harold's first piece by Henry Purcell seemed somewhat tentative, but showed his

---

[3] Loren Glickman was also a contractor who booked jobs in various genres. Luckily for Harold, Loren booked him for a job at Fillmore East, a New York City venue, with Pink Floyd who wanted some brass instruments for their show. It was an exciting experience for Harold, and forever afterward he has delighted in telling all who care that he played with Pink Floyd!

beautiful, lyrical tone. Other selections by Teleman and Tartini seemed more secure. During the last two pieces by Bach it appeared to me that Harold was tired, and his lip was losing control. Nevertheless, he received a standing ovation from this very supportive audience. Afterwards many people stayed to greet the artist and share refreshments.

On the way home Harold expressed his disappointment with his performance.

"I was awful," he said, angrily. "I was so nervous! And I kept seeing Loren there, which made me more nervous! I can't believe I agreed to expose myself like that. And you heard those last two pieces - all fagged out! Terrible!"

"Sweetheart," I began. "I know you were nervous, but your amazingly beautiful tone was there throughout! I knew you were tired at the end, but you've never played alone for so long at a time. People understood that. It's O.K."

"It's not O.K." Harold growled.

"Virginia was thrilled with your playing!" I exclaimed. "I saw Loren and Dobbie talking to you."

"Yeah, I couldn't tell what they really thought, but I can guess!" Harold blared.

"Well, Honey, here we are at home," I said softly.

"What am I going to do?" Harold said gloomily, as he got out of the car, slamming the door as hard as he could.

"You're going to go on, as you always have," I said, grabbing his hand as we walked to the front door of the house. "You'll still play solos on Sundays, and maybe you can bring in a brass quartet some time, even do an evening concert with the quartet and play fewer solo pieces in a row. I know you. This will make you stronger."

"Thanks, Tobe," Harold said, turning on the light in the foyer. I turned it off and flicked the stairway light, as we went upstairs to bed.

Start of Something Big

After touring with Benny Goodman for a year and feeling the pride of playing successfully with the King of Swing, Harold felt somewhat let down and missed the excitement and recognition of playing with a major band. He yearned to continue playing the most prestigious work.

By the late sixties, he had established a solid reputation as a reliable club date player, who could read shows, and he was working in the recording studios and doing jingles, but he had come to New York to achieve success playing all musical idioms - classical, jazz and in between. His goals were to perhaps play with a top symphony orchestra, name bands, and on T.V. and radio shows. He felt stuck, but didn't know where to start.

One night while playing a wedding in one of the catering halls, a man came over to him during a break and said, "What are you doing here?"

Harold thought at first that the man was drunk and said sarcastically, "I was hired to play here," and walked away.

The man followed Harold and said, "You're too good to be playing here. You could do much better."

"Thanks, man," Harold said. "Yeah, maybe your right. Thanks!"

The next day Harold told me about the incident. He said he felt it was a wakeup call that actually kept him up all night trying to figure out how to get out of the rut of club dates and move on to more gratifying jobs.

I remembered how disappointed he was when he didn't pass an audition for the Houston Symphony. He said he was really nervous and Stokowski didn't like his pianissimos. There was no doubt in my mind that Harold had the talent to succeed, but I wondered if he needed a mentor like Armando Ghitalla or a therapist like Dr. Berenda to help him move in a new direction.

Harold thought that was a good idea, and he was able to set up an appointment with Dr. Doris Delgado, a psychologist recommended by the Musician's Union.

The following Wednesday he met with her after he left the union "floor." He told her about his dysfunctional family, his education, his goals and his desire to get ahead in his profession as a trumpet player. When she told him that he needed to schmooze with other musicians at a bar like Joe Harbor's on Broadway and 52nd Street and offer to buy someone like Doc Severinsen a drink, Harold said, "Oh, I can't do that. I'm not good at schmoozing. My hands sweat. I wouldn't make a good impression."

"That's what you need to do to get further in your career in this city. You have to network, get the guys to like you," Dr. Delgado said. "You came to me for help, but you have to make the changes that might get you further. It's up to you! Try it. Go over to Joe Harbor's now and see what happens."

Harold was late coming home because he forced himself to go to the bar, and while he was there he heard some of the guys talking about the contractor, Gerry Alters, needing a trumpet player on the "Arthur Godfrey Show." He called Dr. Delgado, who was still in her office. "Hold on, let me check my file," she said excitedly. "I have his number!" She gave it to Harold and told him to call it right away. "He may still be in his office," she said. Harold called immediately and Gerry answered.

"I hear you need a trumpet player for the "Arthur Godfrey Show," Harold said forth-rightly when Gerry answered.

"That's right," Gerry said. "Can you get over here right away? CBS Studios, 49 E. 52nd Street - third floor. My name's on the door."

"No problem," Harold said. He was able to play for Gerry as soon as they met.

"Of course, you'll have to play for Arthur. Can you be here tomorrow?" Gerry asked.

"Of course," Harold said.

"Come to my office at 1:00. I'll tell Arthur to expect you, and I'll take you to his studio. See you then."

"See you then," Harold echoed. He left in a daze and felt as if he were walking on air. If Godfrey liked his playing, maybe this would be the chance he had been hoping for - the chance to get more prestigious work and accomplish his lifelong goal of making a name for himself in New

York City! Whatever the outcome tomorrow, Harold was certain that he would always remember this day as the start of something big!

Working with Arthur Godfrey

The next day Harold went to Gerry's office at 1:00.

"Come on," Gerry said, "I'll take you to Arthur's studio. I think he'll like you. Just play like you did yesterday. Feeling O.K?" he asked.

"Great!" Harold said.

Gerry entered Arthur's studio. "Arthur, this is Harold Lieberman, the trumpet player I told you about."

"Hi, Harold," Arthur said, picking up his ukulele. Do you know 'Five Feet Two?' "

"Yeah, Arthur," Harold said, as he un-zipped his trumpet case. Arthur's eager expression and casual manner put him at ease. "Let's play it together," Arthur said, tuning up.

Harold matched Arthur's note, and they played the song. When they finished, Arthur

grinned and exclaimed in that deep resonant baritone voice, familiar to his loyal listeners, "That
was great! You're some trumpet player! We can
use you here. You're in!" He extended his arm
and he and Harold shook hands.

"Thanks, Arthur," Harold said. "I'm
thrilled to play with you. I guess I'll see you
soon."

"You sure as hell will," Arthur assured
him with a grin.

Gerry patted Harold's shoulder and said,
"Great, man! Great! You are officially a member
of the 'Godfreymen'! Come on back to my office
and I'll tell you the next step." Gerry motioned
for Harold to sit down. He explained that Harold
would need to meet Lou Schube, the contractor
for the entire staff of CBS musicians.

"Be at my office tomorrow at 1:00. I'll introduce you to Schube, you'll sign some papers,
and you'll be on staff."

"O.K., Gerry!" Harold said excitedly.

"Arthur likes me!" Harold thought. "I'm in!"

He slowly pondered over the implications of his new status - prestige, recognition, stability, a steady salary and a chance to be accepted as a true professional trumpet player. Tomorrow when he met Shube and signed some papers he would be on staff at CBS. This was indeed a major step toward his goal to achieve success in the big city. He was overjoyed!

So, Harold first joined CBS TV and Radio as a trumpeter in 1967, assigned to the Arthur Godfrey radio show, and as a staff member he played with the CBS Symphony when needed, as well as on the Ed Sullivan and Carol Burnett shows on T.V. He remained as a band member until 1972, when all staff musicians at NBC, ABC, and CBS were terminated for economic reasons. In the future freelance musicians were hired as needed.

The Godfreymen consisted of Remo Palmier on guitar, Hal McCusick on saxophone, Andy Fitzgerald on clarinet, Lou McGarrity on trombone, Harold on trumpet, Gene Traxler on bass, Ronnie Traxler on drums and, of course, Arthur who played ukulele and banjo and sang.

Harold was lucky to sit next to Lou who was extremely helpful as mentor and advisor. His first words to Harold were, "If you want to succeed and stay on the show, never call Arthur, 'Art,' never have physical contact with him (shake hands, pat him on the shoulder), never fraternize with the women on the show (Arthur was very possessive) and never utter, 'I used to listen to you when I was a kid.' "

Harold's first month on the job the show went down to the Bahamas to tape a series of programs. Since wives and children were included, I went along. Our son, Aaron, was not yet walking, and I had some trepidation about having to deal with bottles and diapers, naps and general care required of such a young child on an island vacation, but we did want our seven-year-old daughter, Rhonda, to go, so I decided I could manage. Actually, Ronnie and his wife, Nyra, also brought their young son. We soon developed a relationship and their two daughters and Rhonda became friends, spending most of their time frolicking in the pool.

Rehearsals were held in the dining room of one of the hotels where the band stayed. During the rehearsal, Arthur selected "South" - a Dixieland type arrangement of an old classic. Harold played it and everything seemed just fine.

The band took a break and Harold went to the liquor store to buy some wine. He was surprised to see Arthur walk in and said, (forgetting Lou's admonitions) "Hi Art!" It was too late for him to include, "thur," but he couldn't believe he made such a stupid mistake when he was trying so hard to be accepted.

Realizing his profound blunder and knowing that Arthur had flown down to one of the out islands, he sheepishly asked, "Did you fly down to the out island?" Arthur's face reddened and he said, "I sure the fuck didn't swim down."

When Harold returned to the rehearsal, he cornered Lou and whispered what had transpired in the liquor store. "What!" Lou exclaimed. "After I told you never to call him Art!"

Arthur came back to the rehearsal and with banjo in hand blurted out, "Let's rehearse 'South' again and start at the trumpet solo."

Lou whispered, "Give it all you've got, man!"

Arthur listened intently and luckily for Harold, he had passed his audition and remained on the show.

As time went on Arthur was very supportive and unusually warm towards Harold and in
1969, he gave him a picture of himself with the
inscription:

For Harold J. Lieberman. With great admiration.
Sincerely, Arthur Godfrey. 10/13/69.

Gerry Alters, the band leader and arranger
on the show composed and arranged a catchy
flugel horn solo with the band entitled, "The
Love Call of Harold J. Lieberman." Arthur liked
it. The audience response (including fan letters
to Harold) was very favorable, and it got much
air play. From that arrangement on, Harold was
always referred to as Harold J. Lieberman.

Harold's brother, Milton, told Harold that
during the run of the "Arthur Godfrey Show"
their mother, who never understood Harold's
struggles or appreciated his goals, listened faith-
fully to the show and boasted to her friends about

her successful son. Harold didn't really care, having severed all ties with her after their meeting in his therapist's office where her only reaction to his remarks regarding her lack of regard for his feelings or pursuits was to say, "You're not getting a penny from me!"

Walter Cronkite

On one occasion, Harold was asked by the CBS music contractor, Lou Schube, to call Walter Cronkite, a well known network news commentator and host of a Saturday morning TV show called *You are There.* Harold was pleased to have a new assignment and was eager to find out more about it.

The next day, after a friendly introduction, Cronkite asked Harold to sit down and told him that the upcoming episode of his show was entitled "The Pursuit of Pancho Villa." In his mellifluous, resonant, baritone voice, he said excitedly, "picture Villa surrounded by army troops. He is ordered to surrender, and if he doesn't give himself up, the bugler will sound the call of 'no retreat.' Then the armed soldiers will attack him, showing no mercy!"

"That's an amazing situation," Harold

exclaimed. "I can only surmise, since you want me to play a bugle, what the outcome will be!"

"Right," Cronkite agreed. "Now, every detail of this show has to be authentic, so you will play from the actual notated manuscript on the original bugle, which is being obtained from a Mexican museum and will arrive next Monday. So, I want you to plan to meet me in Studio C on Tuesday morning at 11:00 A.M. for a final rehearsal before recording."

"No problem," Mr. Cronkite," Harold said. "It's a real honor!"

On Tuesday after Harold and Cronkite exchanged greetings, Cronkite said excitedly, "Here it is!" He handed Harold a severely dented and misshapen instrument that Harold tried to play, and, much to his horror and embarrassment, produced only a few harsh out of tune notes. Furthermore, the paper on which the actual notated call was supposedly written out contained what showed only incomprehensible washed out notes.

Harold stopped, frowned, shook his head back and forth and looked at the floor, trying to think of a solution.

"Mr. Cronkite," Harold said.

"Go on, Harold, that's a good start! It's really authentic!" Cronkite urged.

"Mr. Cronkite," Harold continued, "I own a wonderful bugle that I used while a bugler at Arlington National Cemetery during my Air Force days."

"Harold," Cronkite interrupted, "that's not an option! Everything on this show must be authentic, beyond reproach," he said emphatically.

Harold had no choice but to play the "Call of No Retreat," as authentically as possible.

When the cue came for Harold to play, he puckered-up and gave it his best shot. He felt he sounded awful with a lifeless tone, missed notes, jagged attacks, faulty intonation and a performance that left him feeling dismal and humiliated.

Cronkite emerged from the control room with a big smile on his face. He approached Harold, exclaiming, "Harold, that was great! That was exactly what I wanted!" He patted Harold on the back and as Harold carefully put the bugle down, Cronkite vigorously shook his hand.

Harold was relieved to leave the studio, never wanting to hear what he had just done.

I did want to hear how Harold managed to make a "purse out of a sow's ear," so I found out the air date, told Harold I was going shopping with a girlfriend on that Saturday morning, went to my friend's house and watched "The Pursuit of Pancho Villa" on *You Are There*. I thought his rendition was splendid!

Impact of Ethical Recital

Following his experience performing for a supportive audience at the Ethical Culture Society in Teaneck, New Jersey, Harold was inspired to find opportunities to play his classical repertoire in other venues, such as churches and libraries.

About this time, Harold met Chris Dedrick, a young musician, composer and arranger who was inspired by Harold to write a piece, "Superimpositions," for piccolo and C trumpet, flugelhorn, strings and the New York Electric Chamber Ensemble, which he dedicated to Harold. The work was premiered in April, 1970, with the Adelphi Symphony Orchestra of New Jersey, conducted by Emmanuel Vardi, a well-known conductor, composer and violist who played under Arturro Toscanini.

With this performance, Harold was building his confidence and endurance, and when he felt ready, he contacted his friend, Joseph Turrin, a fine accompanist, conductor and pianist and together they planned a program which they played in a recital hall at Lincoln Center.

In 1970, now eleven years after his graduation from Juilliard, Harold was not only older, he was wiser, more experienced and very confident that he could meet the more taxing challenge of appearing before an audience in a recital, and he explained his plan to me.

"Tobe," he said, "I've made a decision. I want to give a recital at Carnegie Recital Hall. I've always regretted not giving one at Juilliard, but I really believe that now I can do it! What do you think?" he asked.

"I think you should do it!" I exclaimed. "You've paid a lot of dues to get to this place!" I added.

"I have, haven't I! And now I have the support of some outstanding musicians to join me!" Harold said excitedly. "I'm not going to wear myself out playing a whole program alone like I did at Ethical Culture."

"What do you mean?" I asked.

"Well." Harold told me, "Manny Vardi will conduct a string orchestra during the first half."

"The whole first half?" I interrupted.

"The orchestra will open the concert. Then I'll play two baroque works with the orchestra - a Handel 'Suite in D' and a Tartini 'Concert in D.' "

"You've really been planning!" I observed.

"Practicing and planning!" Harold said with a grin. "After an intermission, all the music will be contemporary. Three pieces have been written for me _ "

"Written for you?" I asked with surprise.

"Am I lucky, or what? Yeah! Richard Peaslee has written a beautiful piece for flugelhorn, strings and harp, called "Nightsongs.'"

"Nice," I mused.

"Joe." Harold began

"Turrin," I said with recognition.

"Right," Harold acknowledged. "He's written two pieces - one for flugelhorn and strings and one for piccolo trumpet which I'll play with the New York Electric Chamber Ensemble. The recital will end with the piece written by Chris Dedrick called 'Superimpositions,' that you already heard."

"That group of two electric guitars, electric bass, keyboard and drums is so unique!" I exclaimed. "I can't wait to see how the audience reacts to it. Where have I been while you've been master minding this incredible extravaganza?"

"By my side, I think," Harold said, whirling me around until we landed on the couch, side by side. "But, as I've said, I've been practicing and planning, totally preoccupied. Today, telling you is the first time I've revealed my plan to anyone, but now I know it's a real plan, and I know I can do it."

"Maybe tomorrow you can tell me how you'll get an audience," I conjectured, elbowing him gently.

"No problem," Harold elbowed back. "For a price, the hall supplies a guy who takes care of that. I just stand in front and perform, which I can't wait to do."

"Perfect," I said, imagining it all.

Carnegie Hall Recital

As we approached Carnegie Recital Hall on Sunday, April 4, 1971, we were excited to see a poster in a glass display case advertising Harold's trumpet recital. It read:

HAROLD J. LIEBERMAN

Trumpet

Music of the

Baroque and Contemporary

Emmanuel Vardi

Conductor of String Orchestra and

The New York Electronic Chamber Ensemble

Sunday 2:30P.M.   Carnegie Recital Hall

April 4, 1971   New York City

I took a picture of Harold next to the display case, and holding hands, we stood looking at the poster for a while, before buzzing for someone to let us in.

This was the big day!

Harold and I were allowed to go into the Hall. I sat in the audience section, already aware of my heart pounding, as if it were to be my recital. I could only imagine how Harold was feeling in anticipation of all the difficult pieces he would be playing and all the trumpet players who would be included in the audience, as well as other well-known musicians, such as Gerry Mulligan, the jazz saxophonist.

While Harold was warming up, playing long tones, routine excerpts from his daily warm ups, and short passages for piccolo trumpet and flugelhorn from pieces in the program, I was admiring his appearance. He was wearing a navy blue double breasted jacket, grey pants and shiny black shoes. We had picked out a beautiful, burgundy tie embossed with subtle swirls. I was so glad he had kept his mustache. I thought it made him look handsome. I hoped my short yellow sleeveless dress wasn't too flashy, but the contemporary styles ruled the day, and were quite different from the more conservative fashions of the 50's.

At about 1:30 a young man in a royal blue sports jacket with a "Carnegie Hall" logo on the pocket came into the Hall to tell us it was time to leave, so the staff could place the orchestra chairs and music stands, check the lights and pick up any stray programs or rubbish left behind at the last recital. He asked me how many seats I would need for any family members. When I told him I would need four, he said he would mark four front row seats "Reserved" for me.

He informed Harold that he could go upstairs to a private room for performers until it was time to begin his recital. Harold thanked him and put his trumpet in its case, as I left my seat in the audience.

"Tobe" Harold said, taking my hand, "this is it. I think I need time by myself."

"I agree," I replied. When I squeezed his hand, it was wet with sweat, an obvious manifestation of the anxiety he was feeling. I hugged him tight. "You'll have this time to meditate (we did transcendental meditation twice a day) and to collect your thoughts. I love you so," I whispered in his ear. "I know you'll play beautifully. This is a highlight of your life, and I'll be with you all the way!"

I let him go, and I went out to the lobby, where I could sit down and just have time to do my own meditation until the doors opened and I could watch for our 10-year-old daughter,

Rhonda, her best friend, Marla, and her mother Harriet, who was driving them from New Jersey. When I spotted them I was so proud of Rhonda dressed in her favorite light blue dress with matching headband circling her beautiful, long blonde hair. I waved to them to join me, so we could go to our reserved seats when the doors opened. They pressed through the crowd, Rhonda rushing into my arms and gushing, "Mommy, I'm so excited. I can't wait to see Daddy!"

(Our four-year-old son, Aaron was home with a baby sitter, but he had been told that Daddy was doing an important "job" playing his trumpet, an explanation he had heard many times before.)

The lobby was beginning to fill with some people I recognized and greeted, and many strangers. The recital billed as "Music of the Baroque and Contemporary," was an unusual combination for a trumpet player, and we expected that by word of mouth many musicians might attend out of curiosity to hear a trumpet player who could play both genres.

The doors opened and I led the way to our reserved seats.

At 2:30 Emanuel Vardi entered from a side door to polite applause. The string orchestra members followed and sat down facing their music stands. The first piece was a short work for strings.

Next, Harold entered the hall and walked confidently to the center of the room acknowledging the applauding audience with a nod. He stepped to the side of the orchestra, glanced at Vardi, placed the trumpet to his lips and played a "Suite in D" for trumpet and strings by Handel, followed by enthusiastic applause. Concluding the baroque section of the recital was "Concert in D" for trumpet and strings by Tartini.

In recognition of a seemingly flawless performance, members of the audience rose to their feet, giving Harold a standing ovation.

Rhonda and Marla were hugging, and Rhonda begged, "Mommy, mommy, can I see Daddy back stage? Please!"

"No, honey, I said, giving her a kiss. "Daddy needs to rest. We'll see him after the concert."

The intermission was a rather chaotic, but exciting time for me. I was pleased to see so many friends from Ethical Culture milling about. Our oldest and dearest friends, the Smiths were smiling and waving to me! They rushed to my side and circled me in a heartfelt embrace. A special treat for me was to reunite with my two friends who had sung with me at Christ Church in lower Manhattan years ago.

I was so proud of Harold and so overcome with emotion to think that, not only our friends, but also this eclectic, energetic crowd was sharing in this special day that Harold had planned and created because of his talent, hard work and determination to conquer his fear of playing in front of a live audience.

The second part of the recital included contemporary rock-influenced works written for Harold by Richard Peaslee, David Spinozza, Joseph Turin and Christopher Dedrick, featuring Harold on piccolo, C trumpet or flugelhorn and all accompanied by the New York Electric Chamber Ensemble. Not only the performances of the talented musicians, but the unique juxtaposition of the two contrasting genres may have generated an excitement in the crowd that brought on unrestrained applause and roused many to their feet, shouting "Bravos!"

Harold had triumphed! He bowed in appreciation and motioned to the musicians to stand, as well as the composers who were seated in the audience.

The gathering dispersed, some to the lobby, others coming forward to congratulate Harold, or speak to other musicians. Rhonda rushed into the throng to embrace her Daddy before I could help her make her way to his side, but eventually he saw her and bent down to give her a hug. Marla and Harriet spoke to Harold before leaving the hall and we thanked Harriet for bringing Rhonda. As soon as we could break away, Harold, Rhonda and I walked to our car. We needed to get home. Harold and I had invited certain close friends to our home in New Jersey, near the George Washington Bridge. Our baby sitter had set out some champagne glasses and light refreshments.

It was hard to let the day go, for Harold

had met a major challenge of his career, and we wanted it to last even after our guests had gone. I don't think we took any pictures, but on Tuesday, April 6, 1971, a review by the music critic, Peter G. Davis, appeared in the *New York Times*. A framed copy hangs in Harold's gallery of treasured reminders of his lifework.

A Setback

In 1971, while hurriedly walking with our four-year-old son on a cold and snowy afternoon, Harold accidentally tripped on a protruding sidewalk grate and fell down, splitting his upper lip. A storeowner witnessed his mishap and offered to drive Harold and Aaron to a nearby hospital where he was kind enough to call me, explaining the situation. When he said, "Your husband split his lip," I said, hysterically, "No, No, you mean my son! My husband couldn't have split his lip!"

I thanked the caller and raced to the hospital where Harold sat in shock, waiting for a surgeon to examine his lip. He eventually received four stitches, and when he asked the doctor how long it would take for his lip to heal, so he could play the trumpet again, the doctor told him that because of the scar tissue that would form, he might not be able to play again. Hearing such bad news, Harold sat slumped over, his hands covering his eyes. I put my arms around him and our little boy and cried. "The doctor could be wrong," Lifting his head and looking at me with tears in his eyes, his face contorted and sad, he said softly, "Tobe, I have to play the trumpet!"

"Mommy, mommy," Aaron whimpered. "Will Daddy be all right?"

"Aaron," Harold said, pulling him to his lap and holding him close,

"I'll be good as new in no time at all."

On the way home I drove through a Dairy Queen and got an ice cream cone for Aaron, and then in silence I pulled into Rhonda's friend's house where she was waiting to be picked up after a bowling date. I had called her from the hospital, so she would be prepared for the shock of what happened, and she bounded into the car. "Daddy, daddy," she cried. "Are you o.k,

Daddy?"

"Daddy fell and hurt his lip!" Aaron shouted.

"I know!" Rhonda said. Their chatter was a welcome interruption to our somber mood until we got home.

But the next six months were heavy times at first, with elephant like sounds coming from Harold's practice room as he began his attempt to recover the use of his lip, in order to rebuild his embouchure.[4] He was determined to play again and never gave up.

When Harold called Arthur, and told him what had happened, Arthur told him not to worry about money and made sure that his checks kept coming in from CBS. Harold consulted various doctors about the scar tissue problem, but they were all doubtful about Harold's full recovery.

---

[4] The fitting of the lips and tongue to the mouthpiece in playing a wind instrument.

However, eventually, Arthur referred Harold to (and paid for) a lip specialist (who had at one time treated Louis Armstrong's damaged lip) to ensure that scar tissue would be kept to a minimum.

In approximately six months, Harold had sufficiently recovered and went back to the show with his lip and embouchure stronger than ever.

Ramapo College

One Sunday morning at the Ethical Culture Society in Teaneck, New Jersey, our speaker was George Potter, an Englishman who had been chosen as president of Ramapo College, a new four year liberal arts college recently opened on spacious grounds, (once a private estate), just outside of Mahwah, New Jersey. This was very good news, as there were at the time few affordable state colleges, and most students were forced to go out of state and pay higher tuitions.

Potter was a man seemingly approaching middle age, of medium height with brown hair cut in a conservative style. He had a dapper appearance and pleasing manner. As he outlined his hopes and plans for this new facility, perhaps his most attractive feature was his impeccable English accent.

During the coffee hour Harold approached Potter and introduced himself, saying that he was impressed with Potter's description of Ramapo College and wondered if there might be a place on the music faculty for him. When he explained that he had degrees from the Juilliard School of Music and Columbia University, Potter asked him where he was presently teaching. Harold mentioned that he had recently done a tour with Benny Goodman and was presently on staff at CBS as a trumpet player on the "Arthur Godfrey Show," as well as playing with the CBS Symphony Orchestra and doing TV productions, such as the Ed Sullivan and Carol Burnett shows; but there were rumors that some time soon there would be an end to hiring staff musicians, as the networks felt it would be more economical to hire freelance musicians instead. Harold told Potter that if and when that time were to come, he would be most interested in applying for a teaching position at Ramapo in the music department, and would especially be eager to incorporate jazz studies in the curriculum.

"Harold," Potter said, extending his hand, "that's a great idea! My wife and I really like jazz and no one on the music faculty covers that specialty. I'm quite impressed with your background and I suggest you call Roger Johnson, who is the head of the music department at the college, to set up an interview. Here's my card with the college phone number, and don't hesitate to call me, as well, whenever you like."

"Thanks, George, meeting you has been an unexpected pleasure! I appreciate your willingness to consider me for the Ramapo faculty. I'll call Roger Johnson next week. I'm very excited about the possibility of teaching at Ramapo!"

When the rumors had started about CBS doing away with staff musicians, Harold began to consider the future. He had become accustomed to the prestige of his staff job and the steady salary it afforded him, especially now that we were a family of four. He could always do four club dates every week end and supplement his income with record dates and jingles, and concerts with "Jazz Impact" the five-piece band he had organized along the way; but after his lip accident, he realized that he could never know exactly what the future would bring if he relied solely on his trumpet playing. He was glad he had taken Tommy Newsome's advice and now had a master's degree. Meeting George Potter and possibly teaching at Ramapo College in the future seemed a stroke of luck.

"What do you think, Tobe?" Harold had asked not long after we heard George Potter at Ethical Culture. "Would you like to be married to a college professor?"

"Can't say I would mind," I said. "Got

it all planned already? Sounds like a wonder-ful life, if you can get it, and you can get it."

"If I try!" Harold interjected.

"I think you would be very spiffy in sweaters and tweed sport coats, standing in front of a class. Just keep me posted, and don't give up your day job until you have to!"

From Show Biz to Academia

In January of 1972, while the musicians were warming up before the rehearsal for the Godfrey Show, Arthur put down his ukulele and said, "Fellas, I'm feelin' really sad, and before we rehearse, I have to tell you something that I just found out from the front office. You guys mean the world to me, and I hate like hell to tell you that the show is going off the air by the end of the summer. There won't be any more staff musicians at all. I wanted to tell you right away, so you can think about your future and have time to make plans."

Chatter from the musicians was immediate but garbled, as each band member reacted to the news with remarks of distress. It was true that there had been rumors that the network planned to eliminate staff musicians for economic reasons, but now it was official and the end was only months away.

As the rehearsal resumed and the usual three shows were taped for the day, Harold felt relieved to know that there might be a teaching job waiting for him at Ramapo College. Now he could call Roger Johnson and tell him that he would be available for the fall term.

When he came home on the last day of the show, he was more subdued than usual. He sat down on the couch, where I joined him with a kiss.

"How are you feeling?" I asked.

"Well," Harold said thoughtfully. "It sure was a good five years and, of course, I'll miss the guys and the challenges, not to mention the prestige and stability, but I think I'm ready to move on.

It was sad for Arthur, though, Harold went on. He announced on the air that it was the last show after 27 years in the same studio at CBS and said he would miss it. (Remo told me later that he had been with Arthur for those 27 years and nothing in the studio had ever been changed, including the drapes.) Arthur said he would be spending more time at his home in Virginia with his family, doing horse shows and flying his airplane.

There were no guests on the shows today. Arthur just wanted to go out playing his ukulele with his band. He closed the last show, saying, 'This is the old red head saying Goodbye,' and we played the theme song, and that was it! Then he said, 'I'll really miss you guys, but what really makes me sad is that after 27 years in this studio no one from the head office has come down to say goodbye.' "

"Did you say anything to him before you left?" I asked.

"Yeah we each went up and said goodbye."

"What did you say, Honey?" I asked.

"I shook his hand and told him what a pleasure it had been to be on the show and thanked him for all the support he gave me when I had my lip accident." Harold said. "I had told everyone about my future plans to teach at Ramapo, and he wished me well."

"So, now in September, instead of heading for the GW Bridge and the CBS studios, you'll be driving up the highway leading to Ramapo College and learning how to be an academic!" I teased.

"Do you think I'll pass the test?" Harold joked.

"Most definitely, silly," I said. "Of course!"

Professor Lieberman

Although Harold was still on staff at CBS, he felt it was important to lay the groundwork for his future after staff musicians were eliminated. He wasted no time calling Roger Johnson, head of the music department at Ramapo College, and was really looking forward to his appointment.

As he drove to the Ramapo campus and was admitted through the gate, he was confident that he would impress Roger with his credentials. He parked his car in the nearest lot and, as he walked on the sidewalk to reach the Arts Building, he was awed by the sheer extent of the grassy fields and vistas of large trees lining the walks and framing the academic buildings. Entering the Arts Building, he located Roger's office and went inside.

A man of medium height with longish

brown hair, wearing a casual shirt and pants, smiled pleasantly, stood and offering his hand introduced himself as Roger Johnson.

Harold enthusiastically shook hands and said, "Great to meet you!"

Roger gestured toward a man with curly hair and of similar height and dress and introduced him as Doctor David Welch, an ethnomusicologist. David got up from his chair, and shook Harold's hand. "It's such a pleasure to meet you!" he said with gusto. They all sat down.

Harold told Roger and David about his meeting with President Potter and their discussion of a possible position in the music department at Ramapo. Roger said that he and David were aware of Harold's experience as a trumpet player and performer with Arthur Godfrey and Benny Goodman, as well as the CBS Symphony.

David remarked that he was impressed with Harold's degrees from Juilliard and Columbia and that his interest in jazz studies would help round out the department.

Harold explained that in the near future for economic reasons the radio-TV networks planned to replace staff musicians with freelance players when needed. He asked Roger if there would be any problem with keeping a spot open for him. Roger assured him that as soon as Harold informed him of his availability, he would tell President Potter, who would take care of any formalities required to place him on the music faculty.

Harold thanked Roger and David and walked buoyantly past the grassy fields and vistas of trees to his car with an overwhelming feeling of euphoria, imagining a whole new life in academia with new colleagues and challenges.

Once again, my multifaceted husband was

ready and able to plunge into yet another adventure that would bring him success.

Jazz Impact

In 1973, Harold met Lynne Kramer, a former actress with a passion to bring arts into the New Jersey public schools through a program she called Project Impact. After hearing Harold play at a fundraiser with his jazz combo, she asked him to lunch where they discussed her interest in adding a jazz ensemble to her project.

Harold was delighted and suggested that the presentation should not only include the performance of jazz music, but a simple oral version of the history of jazz appropriate to the various age groups. The personnel would depend on the musicians Harold was able to book according to the schedule required. A price was negotiated and the group from then on became known as "Jazz Impact."

Harold and I became good friends of Lynne and her husband, Leonard. Lynne told us about her days as an actress. When she mentioned that she was the witch on a Saturday morning radio show called *Let's Pretend*, (popular in the 40's), I was speechless, until I blurted out, "I used to listen to that show back in Iowa every week for years! That was you??? I loved that show!" I'll never forget the visceral jolt and the nostalgia I felt learning that my new friend had been known to me in my childhood in another guise! How special was that!

As time went on, Harold used his favorite professional musicians: (Pianists: Derek Smith, of the "Tonight Show" on NBC or Hank Jones, whom he had met when Hank was a guest on the Godfrey show; Dick Meldonian, a seasoned New York City saxophone player; Sonny Russo, who had played trombone with Frank Sinatra; Linc Milliman, a regular with the Maynard Ferguson band, on bass; and Ronny Bedford, a highly respected sideman on drums) to book jobs in other venues, such as local colleges or various special events. Sometimes the performance included a running commentary narrated spontaneously by Harold; otherwise, the band was simply booked to present a jazz concert.

At one of these events when Hank Jones was trying out the piano before the performance, Harold was shocked by the beat up out-of-tune upright piano on the stage. He found the person in charge and loudly voiced his dissatisfaction. The man's indifferent response when he saw Hank, who is black was, "It's all right for him." As he started to walk away, Harold, interpreting this as a racial slur, lunged at him in a rage and was ready to fight until the other musicians pulled him away. Harold was shaken by the encounter but managed to gain control before the show began.

"Jazz Impact" was so successful that Lynne Kramer suggested that Harold use her as a reference and see if the Sol Hurok talent agency would promote the group, which it did. A six month contract was signed booking the band for concerts in college towns around the country.

The first appearance was to be at Jackson State University in Mississippi, with Derek Smith on piano plus the usual players, with the exception of the bass player, Linc Milliman who was not available. The bass player on this date would be an equally competent musician, Bill Crow.

The group was met at the airport by a personable black woman in a school van who would drive them to the campus.

"Hi, boys! I'm Nellie Carson," she said in a friendly Southern drawl. "Hope you had a good flight. Hop in!" The guys all shook her hand and introduced themselves as they climbed into the van.

Approaching the academic buildings, Harold couldn't help but notice that the students who were walking to class were all black. Why hadn't he been told or why hadn't he realized that a southern university would have mostly black students? His heart sank and his hands began to sweat.

When he got out of the van he caught up with Nellie and asked her if this college was all black.

"Well, yes, it is," she said.

"Wow," Harold stammered. "My band is all white. I should have brought an integrated band to your school!"

Nellie took his hand. "It's o.k. You all just better play pretty good," she said, smiling sweetly.

The fellas tried to reassure Harold that they would play a great concert and the crowd would be sure to appreciate their energy and feeling for the music; but Harold was sullen and worried that the black audience would be disappointed that there were no black musicians in the band. He just couldn't get over his lack of judgement in bringing an all white jazz band to a mostly black university in the state of Mississippi. Nevertheless, when he heard the emcee introduce "Jazz Impact" he strode boldly onto the stage, holding his trumpet under one arm, (seeming to take things in his stride, so to speak) followed by the other brass players carrying their instruments, while Derek, Ronny and Bill went to their instruments which had been set up by the stagehand. They smiled toward the audience, acknowledging the polite applause.

"Good evening," Harold began. "I am Harold Lieberman and this is "Jazz Impact." I would like to introduce the members of the band: on piano, Derek Smith, on saxophone, Dick

Meldonian; trombone, Sonny Russo; on drums Ronny Bedford and on bass," (and he drew a blank and couldn't remember the bass player's name). The bass player loved practical jokes and this was an opportunity too good to pass up.

"JIM," he called out. Harold, by now totally flustered, echoed - "JIM er, ah - JIM CROW! The band members started to laugh. The audience members talked among themselves.

It took Harold a few minutes to realize his humiliating faux pas, but he had to go on. "We'd like to begin the first set with a Charlie Parker tune, 'Scrapple from the Apple,' " he announced with genuine fervor, and they were off! Tune after tune was met with whistles and loud applause. Each individual solo was greeted by appreciative scattered clapping, and Derek's energetic piano solos brought standing ovations. The evening was a huge success and people gathered near the stage to show their appreciation. Harold saw Nellie in the wings giving a "thumbs up," cancelling out all his negative thoughts. Jazz was truly a positive force that had reached the Jackson State crowd regardless of the color of the messengers!

They had been a smash! Recalling the night, Harold would say it had been "dynamite" (a favorite adjective he liked to use for the ultimate best).

The band was like a well-oiled machine - like a champion baseball team, but it was also its own example of professional jazz musicians who loved what they were doing in their own groove.

"Jazz Impact" had many such nights on the Sol Hurok gigs and in other venues for a good twenty years. For Harold, the sweet memories of those days will remain in his secret treasure chest for the rest of his life.

Doc Severinsen Saves the Day

Harold joined the faculty of Ramapo College full time in 1972, and remained there for 29 years. He was not only an educator who could teach jazz improvisation, but he became an innovator. He created a summer jazz workshop with a highly trained faculty for students and adults that included evening concerts open to the community, with local professional musicians and well known soloists, such as Maynard Ferguson, the trumpeter (known as the "high note king") and Buddy Rich, the drummer, drawing huge crowds to the campus and enhancing the reputation of the college.

The night of the Maynard Ferguson concert the crowd was so large that a riot broke out when it became clear that not everyone could get in. The uproar was so intense that Harold spoke to Maynard and announced that there would be a second show for the overflow crowd. Since

Harold was able to resolve the situation peacefully, a possible row was averted and the evening was a success.

One summer Woody Herman and his band were in residence, giving students the opportunity to take lessons with working professionals and attracting a large crowd for the closing concert. Another time the saxophonist, Gerry Mulligan, visited the campus and interacted with the workshop students, as well as performing with his band (which included Harold) in an outdoor setting, again enticing a large crowd.

Harold had the respect of President Potter, as well as the administrators who had input regarding the funding of various projects on campus, and when he proposed that a band shell be built to allow him to produce a series of outdoor concerts, (for which he often conducted and/or performed) he had their full support. Concert themes varied from classical pieces, show tunes or jazz, as well as a patriotic 4th of July annual event when fireworks were dramatically coordinated with the playing of the "1812 Overture." During Harold's tenure, a concert featuring a new president of the college narrating "Peter and the Wolf" was done in a professional manner and was well received.

An unsettling night for Harold happened during a jazz concert featuring the famous singer, Anita O' Day. When she met him at the band shell she told Harold she had to leave after the first set and she wanted her money before she performed. That was news to Harold, but when she finished and left, he went to the mike, shrugged his shoulders, palms up and said, "I thought she was gonna play a whole concert, but she has to catch a plane, so she had to leave." Unlike the Maynard Ferguson crowd, luckily, this one was more mellow, and there were no re-percussions.

Harold's classes were well attended, and his reputation as a lecturer and advisor to his students became firmly established. By the third year at Ramapo he felt ready to apply to be a full professor. The first step in the process began with the approval of his unit, "Contemporary Arts," which he easily received. Next he appeared before the All College Committee where questions were asked to establish his qualifications. Since he didn't have a PHD, he could ask to have his life experience as a professional musician considered. The committee approved his request unanimously. The final interview was with President Potter, who was most cordial when Harold met him in his office.

"Harold," he said, shaking Harold's hand and motioning for him to sit down, "you have received excellent reports from your colleagues and students and your musical events have brought hundreds of people from the community to the campus. I've personally appreciated all you've done in this regard."

Harold smiled and nodded, saying, "Thanks, George."

"Yes," George added, "Ramapo's reputation has definitely benefited! There is no doubt in my mind that you would make an outstanding full professor, but since you've been approved on the basis of your life experience, I just want to follow up on that. For instance, do you think you play as well as Yehudi Menuin?"

"Well. George, Menuin is a violinist. I am a trumpet player. I don't know that I could be compared to him," Harold replied.

"Hmmm," George considered the matter. "Lori (George's wife) and I watch the "Tonight Show." Would you say you are as good as Doc Severinsen?"

"I have played with him. I think I'm almost as good as he is. It's hard to judge my own playing," Harold said.

"Well, Harold, George asked, "Can you get a letter from Doc Severinsen evaluating your playing?"

"Actually, I'm sure I can," Harold answered confidently.

"Good," George said enthusiastically. "See my secretary on the way out and have her set up an appointment for us, say, in two weeks. Hopefully, you'll have some information that will be helpful to me in making a decision about you becoming a full professor. I feel that I need a written recommendation from a famous professional contemporary musician to convince me that your life experience in your field has been on the highest level and is recognized by an expert."

"Of course, I understand," Harold said.

"I'll write to Doc right away."

Harold decided to write to his old Air Force buddy, Tommy Newsome, who was an arranger and assistant conductor to Doc on the "Tonight Show." He explained how important it was for Doc to write as soon as possible to President Potter, (address included) hopefully influencing him to guarantee Harold's promotion to full professor. While he anxiously awaited the two weeks until his appointment with Potter, realizing how ludicrous it might seem to Tommy and Doc that such a letter would make a difference, nevertheless, he hoped Doc would respond and that Potter would make a favorable decision.

When Harold kept the appointment, George got right to the point.

"Well, Harold, he asked. "Do you have a letter from Doc Severinsen?"

"I was hoping you would have it," Harold replied, almost reverting to a stutter.

Just then, the office door opened and George's secretary came in waving an envelope.

"Excuse me, President Potter, but this just came to my desk, and I think it might be important to Harold's situation."

As Potter opened the envelope and began to read the letter out loud, Harold began to relax, feeling that Doc's remarks would be a cinch to influence Potter to move forward with his promotion.

The letter was scrawled in long hand on stationery with a "Tonight Show" letterhead, dated March 2, 1977, and appears below:

"Dear Sirs,

It is my pleasure to indicate to any persons who may be concerned that I have known a fine relationship with Harold Lieberman in a professional capacity.

Mr. Lieberman's fine playing speaks for

itself, but I would like to remind those interested parties that he has a splendid academic background and approach not only to trumpet playing but to all forms of music endeavor.

More important - I believe Hal can impart this musicianship through a fine personality.

I would recommend him most highly as a person, musician and trumpet player.

Sincerely,

Doc Severinsen"

"Harold," Potter remarked, as he handed the letter to Harold to read for himself. "That's what I needed! But here's a letter from someone else." Again, Potter read it out loud.

"Dear Sir:

I have known Harold Lieberman for 25 years. He is an individual of fine moral character and great determination. He is also one of the finest trumpet players in the country; an extremely versatile instrumentalist, ranging from virtuoso type solos in the legitimate field to jazz improvisation and playing lead trumpet in big band ensembles. His professional playing experiences include recording, television, radio, CBS staff orchestra, Arthur Godfrey Show, jazz concerts, clinics and solo appearances.

His educational background includes study at Hartt College in Hartford, Conn., Juilliard and Columbia University. In addition, his experience as teacher, clinician and lecturer on the history of jazz, qualify him for unlimited advancement in the field of education.

Harold and I have been associated musically, socially, professionally, and even on the tennis courts, and I whole-heartedly recommend him.

Very truly yours,

Tommy Newsome

Assistant Conductor

NBC Tonight Show Orchestra"

"I must say I am really impressed and encouraged by these two letters, Harold. They have given me the confidence I wanted to be sure I could promote you to full professor based on your life experience. We'll move ahead now, and my secretary will notify you when the promotion is finalized."

"Thanks, George!" Harold exclaimed. "You must know how happy I am about this promotion!"

"You deserve it, Harold! You're already an outstanding member of our faculty. Best of luck in the future." He and Harold shook hands and Harold left George's office feeling jubilant, wanting to jump and shout for joy.

When he got home and described the scenario that took place in George's office to me, we jumped and shouted for joy together. When we calmed down, we sat on the couch and had a glass of wine, and Harold and I talked about how far he had come.

"I'm so proud of you!" I cried out.

"Thanks, Tobe, Harold said, putting his arm around my shoulders and sitting very close. "Today, knowing that I'll be a full professor has made me think of the image I had growing up and the obstacles I've overcome. I stuttered, my hands sweated, I was overweight, I felt like a failure in school, and..."

"You even lost your lip when you were in the Air Force Band," I murmured.

"Until I met Ghittala and then Dr. Berenda and then I met you." Harold said.

"Yes, and then I met you, I echoed." I gave him a dreamy look. "And then Rhonda and Aaron."

We toasted each other with our wine

glasses and a lingering kiss. "And then Dr. Delgados helped me and I started going to Joe Harbor's bar," Harold continued, "to schmooze with other professional musicians."

"And you got Gerrry Alter's name and learned that Arthur Godfrey needed a trumpet player," I added.

"And then those wonderful stable five years with Godfrey!" Harold proclaimed.

"And now academia," I sighed happily.

"And now Full Professor Harold J. Lieberman," Harold shouted proudly.

"Just don't get too full of yourself, Harold J.," I said with a giggle.

"No chance of that with you to remind me," Harold joked.

"Never mind!" I said. "I'm sure you will continue to amaze me!"

"I'll do my best" Harold said, having the last

word.

Transition

In 1980, I was a teacher at Friends Neighborhood Nursery School, a Quaker school in Ridgewood, New Jersey. Ten years later, I became the owner of The Music Learning Place, a music studio for four and five year olds (which included movement to music and games involving rhythmic patterns and ear training, reinforced with percussion instruments and simple exercises at keyboards). Eventually, I limited my practice to giving five to twelve year olds private piano lessons in my home. I thoroughly enjoyed my work, but after a while I felt burned out and was ready to retire.

Coincidently, after teaching at Ramapo College for 29 years, Harold told me he wanted to take early retirement. He made inquiries and learned that we could continue our health benefits, and the only requirement would be to complete a project of some kind or give a master lecture on an unusual subject. He said he preferred to give a lecture and was already doing research to choose a suitable topic.

I composed a letter announcing my retirement. As soon as Harold's plans were definite, I would send it. I was relieved to know we were both ready to move in a new direction.

In 1999, when Harold became certain that he wanted to apply for early retirement, he began to search for a suitable subject for a lecture. While surfing the internet, he came upon a band called Charlie's Orchestra playing swing music in the style of Benny Goodman. Harold had played with Benny in the 60's, and he knew the band he was hearing was not the Benny Goodman band, because he detected what he could only describe as an "accent." Further research yielded information that Charlie's band was a propaganda tool used by the Nazi Propaganda

Ministry during the Third Reich to demoralize American forces.

Harold was fascinated with this phenomenon and after delving into the subject further and also finding authentic Nazi films, posters and photos, he decided to present as fulfillment of the requirement for early retirement a multimedia lecture entitled "Jazz as Propaganda in the Third Reich." His proposal was accepted and his lecture, sponsored by the Ramapo College Center for Holocaust and Genocide Studies, was scheduled to be presented to the Ramapo Community, as well as the general public, on the Ramapo Campus at the Berrie Center for Performing and Visual Arts at 7:00P.M. on May 9, 2000.

I arrived on the campus about 6:00 and went to Harold's office, where he was going over his notes.

"Hey!" he exclaimed, as I leaned over to

give him a kiss.

"Hey, yourself!" I echoed. "How are you feeling?" I asked.

"Fantastic!" he replied. "I'm ready and eager to wow 'em!"

"Great! I just wanted to see you. I'm going to the Berrie Center to people watch as they come in. You seem relaxed, and I know you'll outdo yourself! See you later!"

As I walked to the Berrie Center, I felt a certain sadness come over me, knowing that this would be Harold's last hurrah at Ramapo and the end of any official connection to the campus community we had both enjoyed for almost thirty years; but when I entered the lobby and saw a few faculty members who greeted me warmly I became more grounded in the present. I looked forward to Harold's lecture with an inner feeling of contentment, knowing that not only his friends and colleagues would be in the auditorium, but also our children, Rhonda and Aaron[5]

Harold was introduced by the newest member of the music faculty, Mack Brandon, who praised him as a caring mentor to his music students (and he added shyly, to Mack himself) and for the fine legacy he had left to the college and the larger surrounding community with the concerts he produced through the years.

Harold had a relaxed, easy going stage presence and he spoke in a pleasant and well-modulated voice. His enthusiasm for his subject

---

[5] After graduating from the Jane Adams School of Social Work in Chicago, Rhonda moved to New Jersey and worked in a mental health center as a therapist. When Harold and I went to her graduation, she was able to show us the room and chair where Benny Goodman had taken his first clarinet lessons at Jane Adams' Hull House, a settlement house where underprivileged children could receive free lessons.

Aaron graduated from the Manhattan School of Music with a concentration in Jazz Studies and guitar. He became a founding member of a rock band called "God Street Wine" that had a successful ten years touring, performing and recording for Geffen and Mercury Records. Later he moved to New York City and worked as a freelance musician continuing Harold's legacy.

comfortably held the attention of his audience. In his lecture, Harold did a superb job of presenting the material that initially fascinated him. The accompanying multimedia items were coordinated seamlessly by computer to a large screen above the stage. Nazi films, including images of Hitler and soldiers marching in goose step with swastika flags flying and adoring countrymen saluting by raising right arms toward the Fuhrer, set the stage for the audience. Pictures of anti-Semitic posters were disturbing, but the effect was electric and impressive. Photographs of the studio where Charlie's Orchestra made their recordings provided authentic local color, and hearing the actual recordings using familiar jazz songs with mocking lyrics brought the evil intent alive.

Overall, Harold's skillfully constructed lecture and the unusual subject matter it covered brought a standing ovation at the conclusion, and he was surrounded in the lobby by those wishing to congratulate him. On a table was a beautiful glass free standing plaque with the engraved words:

Presented to

Professor Harold Lieberman

Congratulations on your much-deserved retirement.

Bravo to you

From your colleagues

at Ramapo College

May 9, 2000

Also on the table was a large leather notebook with the inscription, "Professor Harold Lieberman" on its cover, which contained personal messages from colleagues and blank pages for others who wanted to be included. Harold beamed in appreciation, and the many conversations among friends and enthusiastic personal words of congratulations and praise to Harold created a joyful and memorable celebration.

Retirement

Naomi and Jesse Kahan, whom we originally met in Englewood, New Jersey, eventually moved to Ridgewood, looking for better schools for their children, as we had done. We often met for dinner, and one evening we discussed trips and vacation spots. They told us that for years they had taken their family to Sanibel Island, Florida, for two weeks every winter. Their enthusiasm for the beautiful Gulf of Mexico beaches, good restaurants and cultural events motivated us to go the same two weeks in 1998.

Harold felt that Sanibel was an ideal place to retire and wanted to look for a place to buy. After consulting with several realtors, we bought a condo in Donax Village, within walking distance of the beach. We sold our house in New Jersey, and bought a condo in Maverick Knolls in Woodstock, N.Y. We could now be snowbirds and have the best of both worlds -sunny Sanibel in the winter and the beautiful Hudson Valley in the spring, summer and fall.

In Sanibel, we quickly discovered BIG ARTS (BARRIER ISLAND GROUP FOR THE ARTS), a center for art classes, concerts, current event discussions, lectures, plays and movies. There was always something to do and new people to meet. Our days were full. We swam in the pool, Harold played tennis, we walked long stretches of beaches and learned the "Sanibel Stoop," (an expression coined by 'who knows who?' and 'who knows when?') for those who stopped to collect the many shells washed onto Sanibel's Gulf shore. I took watercolor classes, got lots of paints and brushes, met like-minded people (mostly women), learned by imitating demos of whatever teacher led the class. Harold eagerly offered himself as a lecturer and presented his "Jazz as Propaganda" program, "Women in Jazz" series, and the "Swing Era." We attended current events meetings, various lectures, book clubs, plays, movies and concerts that included string quartets, classical and jazz soloists, classical orchestras and jazz bands, as well as dance groups.

Everywhere we went we met more and more new people, some of whom, became close friends, as did a nucleus of neighbors at Donax Village. One of those neighbors saw an ad in the *Sanibel Times* looking for a music critic for the paper. Harold applied and was given the position. As we went to all the concerts anyway, it was easy for Harold to take notes at the concerts. The hard part was staying up for hours afterwards to write the reviews, which I then sleepily edited the next morning, so they could be on the editor's desk as soon as possible. This was a small town and the many people who went to the concerts began to read the reviews and soon Harold (whose byline and picture accompanied each one) became recognized and respected for his reviews. People began to include us in their dinner parties and spoke to us on the street or at the beach. Life was good!!

When we went back to Woodstock we were slowly integrated into the Maverick Knolls community and began making friends there. We went to the outdoor Maverick Concerts and when we discovered nearby Bard College, a liberal arts college with no football team, but a music conservatory and many concerts and some operas and plays, we were thrilled!

Soon we found out about "Lifetime Learning" at Bard, where Harold was able to do lectures. Later he also lectured at a lifetime learning group called "Lifespring," in a nearby community.

Harold is a natural born storyteller with a droll sense of humor and during his run as a jazz musician he met many well-known musicians, giving him a rare repertoire of anecdotes that people look forward to hearing (such as never knowing if Benny (Goodman) 'Bad Man' might fire you; meeting Louis Armstrong, who gave him a tin of salve for chapped lips that he shows his classes; Clark Terry, the great jazz artist who loaned Harold $400.00 in cash so we could go to Atlantic City one day after the banks were closed; Walter Sear, a composer and tuba player who pioneered the Moog Synthesizer and loaned Harold part of the money for a down payment on our first house; Arthur Godfrey who, contrary to rumors, was not anti semitic, was an environmentalist and paid for Harold's lip surgery after an accident and kept his salary coming at CBS until he could play again; and all the talented people Harold was privileged to meet, like Mel Torme', who never took a lesson in his life, but sang, played and wrote songs ("Chesnuts Roasting on an Open Fire," etc.) and played drums; Vic Damone, who told Harold that he sang for God; Dizzy Gillespie who picked up our two year old, Rhonda, in a produce store in Englewood, N.J., where we all once lived; Laura Nero at a record date, Pink Floyd, when he was contracted by our neighbor, Loren Glickman, the bassoonist with Mostly Mozart, to play a date at Fillmore East; just to mention a few examples of the many stories that Harold loves to recall, even sometimes to a clerk at a deli or to a new friend. He sincerely loves an audience and always uses the Godfrey style of speaking as if to one person. After his lectures his audience usually show their appreciation by smiling, applauding or giving him standing ovations. I think that's why, no matter how many times I have heard his lectures, I go to every one, just to see how happy he is sharing information and stories with each audience. Then I go home happy too, because I love the man.

Ron Howard Meets "The Old Trumpet Player"

Although we were very content with our life style in Sanibel, I did miss Rhonda and Aaron, who only visited us a few times, and I missed the East Coast in general. Harold was becoming disillusioned with the caliber of the concerts he reviewed and when a young, inexperienced editor was hired, he no longer enjoyed the job. We began to feel that perhaps we had enough of Florida and considered selling our condo.

In 2003, when Aaron told us his girlfriend, Aimee, and he were planning to get married and move to the Hudson Valley, where they hoped to start a family, I realized I wanted to leave Florida and make our New York State residence in Woodstock our only home. Since Harold understood my need and was also ready to leave Sanibel, we put our condo up for sale. It took us three years to sell it, but we were in Woodstock when Aaron and Aimee got married in June, 2004, and on November 4, 2007, for the birth of their fraternal twins, Milo and Delilah.

Our daughter, Rhonda, a manager of social workers at the Children's Hospital of Montefiore Hospital in the Bronx, lived in Riverdale, N.Y., only about an hour away from Woodstock. We could be a family again!

Aaron was working as a music teacher at a private school in Poughkeepsie, N.Y., when he heard that "The Metropolitan Hot Club" (a spin off group of a gypsy band led by Django Reinhardt in the 20's,) was looking for a guitar player. He contacted Michael Boyle, the leader and became a member of the group. The instrumentation of two guitars, standup bass and violin and the novelty of the jazzy 20's music appealed to those who found the band's website, and they began to get bookings for weddings, parties, restaurants and concerts in libraries and art galleries. Aaron had developed his voice during ten years on the road with the rock band," God Street Wine," and he was not only able to sing in the rock idiom, but he could also sing a ballad sensitively and tenderly, which added variety to the Metropolitan Hot Club's performances.

By 2007, when Harold was in his seventies, enjoying his retirement and no longer practicing the trumpet, Aaron called him to say that his band had a job at the Rosendale Cafe, near Woodstock.

"Dad," he said. "The band wants you to sit in with us!"

"Aaron, I can't do that. I haven't practiced for over a year!"

"You can do it, Dad," Aaron urged. "Our booking is a month away."

"I'll try," Harold said reluctantly, "but I don't guarantee that I'll sound very good."

The band drew a sizable crowd to the Rosendale Cafe for their appearance. Harold was featured as a guest artist, and when he played the crowd paid attention, clapping and sometimes shouting their approval. He may not have been at the peak of his powers, but his years of experience and his professionalism were evident and appreciated. The owner of the club made a video of the performance that the band put on you-tube and was noticed by the actor and producer, Ron Howard, whose daughter was getting married and looking for a band for the wedding reception.

Harold got a call from Aaron - "Dad! Are you ready for this?"

"What?"

"Michael got a call from Ron Howard, the movie producer. He wants our band to play at his daughter's wedding in Greenwich, Conn., but he especially wants the old trumpet player! Can you believe it?"

"You want me to play again? Aaron, I told you I don't practice anymore. I sounded terrible."

"Dad, you've got to do it! We can make a lot of money and he said he'd pay extra for you."

"O.K., O.K. Book it. I'll do my best."

At the wedding reception, the band was a hit with the Howard family and their guests, who danced with abandon to the lively tunes. During a break, Harold was able to have a pleasant conversation with Ron Howard, who asked Harold if he could play like Louis Armstrong. He complied by including his rendition of "What a Wonderful World," (complete with vocals) during one of the sets, receiving enthusiastic applause and cheers.

The ride to and from the job was a rare

time for Harold and Aaron to bond and important for them both. Aaron was grateful to Harold for enhancing the band, and Harold was satisfied that he had been able to play adequately.

This was the last time he played the trumpet. He had practiced every day of his life from age thirteen into his sixties, and by the 21st Century he was content to spend time with his family and friends and to give occasional lectures. As Harold would say, he had a "wonnaful" (sic) and amazing career and had no regrets.

Afterthoughts

Harold had a long and successful career as a jazz trumpet player and educator. He also played classical music as a soloist and in recitals and brass quintets.

Having grown up in a dysfunctional family, Harold's response to stress at home caused him to stutter and his hands to sweat. These conditions plagued him into adulthood, but his first means of relief was to play the trumpet, and his perseverance to excel moved him further and further ahead toward deliverance from his shortcomings. He was fortunate to meet mentors who encouraged him to believe in himself. He did the work and had the talent to fulfill his dream to be a trumpet player in New York City.

In addition to that accomplishment I can tell you that he and I found each other quite by accident, fell in love, and through the hard work of communication and compromise have sealed our commitment to each other at this time for fifty-eight years.

Post Script:

Harold needed a practice room in our house. He singlehandedly did the work to convert our unfinished basement into a comfortable living space, including a soundproof room where he could practice. He said that it only takes one nail at a time.

It occurs to me that could be a metaphor for his life. It seems to have brought him many rewards.

Acknowledgements

I am grateful to Gerry Alters for writing the song whose title I have used for this book.

I want to thank my husband, Harold J. Lieberman for the life we share and for the trust he had in me to chronicle his career, being willing to accept my request that he not read the text until it made it to publication. He was always there to clarify dates and facts, but the writing is my own.

My deepest loving appreciation to my daughter, Rhonda Joy, for her constant advocacy for all my endeavors.

My dear son, Aaron, has relieved me of all responsibilities for the technical support needed to complete this project, and for that I am extremely grateful.

Without Beverly Sloane, writer, teacher, writing coach and friend, who encouraged me every step of the way, this book would never have been written. She said I was a writer, and I was able to begin to believe it.

I feel enormous gratitude for the support of Ruth Levine who saw the whole picture and kept me going.

I am honored that Bill Crow and Phil Shoptaugh were willing to read the manuscript and to comment on the book.

Sincere appreciation to Fran Wishnick, author of "Craig Climbed a Tree," for her generous sharing of her experience with self-publishing.

Made in the USA
San Bernardino, CA
20 June 2017